BECOMING AN
INFLUENTIAL
LEADER

How to Gain and Sustain it With Others
In Your Generation

DR. SAMUEL ODEKE, DSL

Contents

Dedication

This book is written to shine light on the over 7 billion people God has placed on Earth,regardless of their socio-economic status, culture, upbringing, or political system they find themselves.. I believe that there is an answer to this question, and that none of them were created by accident. Instead, God has a purpose for every one of them, and I believe he desires for each of them to have a tremendous impact on their generation.

Tragically, in spite of this potential, majority of them will go through life without achieving anything substantial other than making a living to survive and then die, having lived a life that had little more effect than a pebble tossed into the ocean. After death, they will be placed in "a plot" somewhere in their homeland, which we all know as either a grave or cemetery. Then eventually, their bodies will decay and they will become food for worms.

To my family and friends reading this book, please know that you have huge untapped potentials. You are pregnant with gifts and if you believe in yourself more than your culture or tradition, God will make your dreams a reality and enable that dream or vision to come to fruition.

If God gives you a vision, it will be fulfilled if you submit and believe. If God showed you a "Promised Land," it will be manifested. Man cannot cancel God's purposes. if you fail to do what he called you to do, he will get somebody else and you will be the one who misses out on the purpose for which you were made. Only you can cancel that mission you were selected to do because of your fear, irresponsibility, inconsistency and other factors. Success in every vision requires God's principles to be upheld and never violated.

To my family, you have always been the greatest gift that God gave me. I believe that God will continue to use you more than ever. You will do more significant works because God has placed that ability within you. I trust that you will study, learn and apply the biblical laws and principles taught in this book to make the world a better place and make a difference in your generation. I pray you will be consistent and responsible during your time here on Earth. This book is a result of commitment and hard work. I spent many a sleepless night seeking God as I strove to put these principles together.

To the Source of all things and creation, the Alpha and Omega, my eternal Father and God Who does things according to His purpose and for a purpose. You gave me the gift of life so I could be a blessing in my generation and for those who come after me when my assignment during this Earthly journey is complete and I depart this mortal coil. May the truths that I discovered in your Holy Word explode in the hearts of every man and woman who reads this book. May you inspire them to apply these principles throughout their lifetime. Let these principles stick and constantly remind them as they pursue their dreams and visions. It is possible with you, as Our God, to achieve all that you wanted for us before time began. My prayer is that every person created in God's image discovers and goes on to do the most important thing that makes a difference or an impact in the world for the benefit of the next generation.

Acknowledgement

I would like to appreciate the support of my friends and family towards making this dream come true. My desire is to help others and I too need help. My family and friends have actually provided that support.

I also want to thank my editor, Mr. Samuel. O. Adeyemi of *Media DNA* in Lagos, Nigeria for the gift and skills that you possess. I am indebted to you all for the support you have extended to me. Also, I want to appreciate Emmanuel Ayo Oshewolo, the cover designer for the job well done. You have believed in me and believed in my vision to make the world a better place so that the next generation does not miss out on what we are supposed to accomplish before we die. Our inconsistency and irresponsibility should not cause the next generation to lose their blessings and their inheritance.

Without the final insight from Dr.Jason Newcomb, this work would still have some gaps and potential errors. You are very special to me. Thank you for final review of the manuscript. I believe that you are gifted in editing and I believe it will bring you before great men. God's says those words in Proverbs 19:16

Without God leading me through life, I would not have come to a level of thinking about writing these ideas down in a book and sharing them with you. I believe that these ideas and knowledge will make you a very different person that will enable you to impact your generation if you follow and apply them. I have come from very far in life; the road has been filled with adventures of mountains and valleys. There have been thick forests, flat, sandy and open spaces along the journey. I thank God the Almighty, Alpha, and Omega for everything that He has done in my life and for lifting me from a little unknown rural village in Uganda.

Foreword

I first met Dr. Samuel Odeke at our doctoral graduation ceremony on May 6, 2017. When I was younger, I believed naively in coincidences. I'm here to tell you that Samuel and I seated next to one another was no coincidence. Since our graduation and meal together, Samuel and I have developed a friendship built primarily through emails. We have helped one another. We have prayed for one another. Not only were we treated to a graduation experience that felt more like worship, but also some caring professors created a dining experience for several of us. Our professors encouraged and inspired us students to do more. Let me say to you that Samuel does not and has not taken that charge lightly.

I once wrote Samuel and asked if he ever slept! He churns out leadership materials such as this book and others in addition to working his regular work hours and balancing time with his family. He is driven. He is motivated. Better yet, he lives and breathes what he shares and teaches. He is a servant at heart. I genuinely believe he puts out so much work to help others. He works tirelessly to provide materials to share with the world. Samuel shares what has helped him overcome adversity. He takes the things he found useful, pairs that with his educational and work experiences, and then shares those principles to help you, the reader. He does this in a way that provides value to others while also glorifying the lord. In short, Samuel's teachings are practical and grounded in personal and Biblical experiences.

If you meet Samuel, you will realize fairly quickly he is an encourager. You likely will be greeted with a smile and quite possibly a hug. His positivity and joy for life is obvious. His love for his family is strong. It is his faith, however, that I believe is the most touching thing about him. It will be clear to you his relationship with Jesus Christ is the most important thing to him. Samuel does everything he can to provide value to you while also glorifying the Lord. His passion combines his unique experiences, knowledge, skills, and abilities along with Biblical principles to give you a solid foundation to create positive changes in your life to be a better leader.

My friend Samuel says, "Trapped inside every person is a leader." Samuel truly wants to help free your leader. He doesn't just talk about it. He walks you through the process that helped him be the leader he is today. He provides you steps, examples, and encouragement. Please don't misunderstand. Samuel doesn't sugarcoat things. Instead, he tells you what to expect as you begin to make positive changes for yourself. The path to leadership often isn't easy; however, Samuel does his best in making things clear for you.

In his work, Samuel talks about the power of personal gifts and seeds. Through this book, Samuel uses his gifts to help you not only discover your gift and seed inside you, but also to help you grow and develop them. He challenges and encourages you to share your gift with the world, but he doesn't just stop there. He guides you through starting your leadership discovery, developing a personal plan, and even helping your replacement as you step away from leadership. In other words, Samuel guides you throughout the lifespan of leadership. He does this using clear examples and stories. You will learn lessons effortlessly with Samuel's conversational writing style. Samuel does not just want you to become a great leader; he also wants to help you be a better person.

The way I see it, Samuel believes if he can do it, you and I can, too. He has overcome adversity and knows what it takes to help you do the same. Personally, I have been touched by his stories. I have recalled some of his experiences to help me overcome bouts of negativity and discouragement in my own life. I have been touched by his positivity. In the seven months I have known him at the time of this writing, I have grown as a person and a leader thanks to Samuel. As you read, I believe you will grow as well.

In other words, Samuel does his part. Now, it's time to do yours. Read on and be blessed. Let Samuel help you be the leader (and person) you were meant to be.

Dr. Jason Newcomb, LCPC
Counselor
Regent University '17
December 30, 2017

Preface

Why Another Book On Becoming An Influential Leader?

There have been hundreds or thousands of books written on the subject of leadership by different scholars and practitioners over the ages. Even when I started to write this book, that thought came into my mind, and for several months I was praying for an answer or answers as to what would make this book different and important. I believe I was able to get my answer. You might not believe in prayer, but for now let me share my thoughts: Have you ever wondered why companies like, Apple, Samsung, Sony, or Toyota make new products? To me the answer is simple, they are pursuing their mission, vision and purpose.

The Following Are The Reasons For This New Book On Leadership:

1. This book provides fresh perspectives on leadership and true principles on why we need leaders. The world is facing global problems such as terrorism, poverty, political confusion, bad leadership and diseases. It also helps resolve some of the political, social, economic, psychological and spiritual problems we see today. We need leaders who can influence the world to make it a better place for peaceful co-existence.

2. This leadership book is filled with fresh ideas on the subject of leadership. Leadership has been around since the beginning of mankind, and the Greek thinkers were the first to write

their thoughts on the subject. They went on to influence millions of people over the years. We and the generations before us have followed, applied and believed in those ideas about leadership, seldomly questioning them. This book attempts to challenge those concepts or views about leadership.

3. The world has millions of people who need practical wisdom which is useful for our future leaders. To live effectively, you need knowledge. If a person has money but no good sense, that person will remain ineffective. Knowledge is necessary for survival. Put another way; wisdom is the key to life.

4. There are millions of people who are hopeless, and that is why people are committing suicide, killing each other and fighting for leadership positions, status, power, and have lost their direction or significance. This book will inspire people to discover their leadership abilities that I believe every human being possesses.

5. This book is also filled with knowledge which are essential and relevant for a better understanding of what leaders do, how to become a leader, the process of becoming a leader, the price to pay, and how to increase leader's values to lead effectively and make a difference.

6. This book has wellsprings of knowledge by providing a stream of ideas, concepts, points, knowledge and insights that can enable people to discover their leadership capacity and impact their generations. The word wellspring is chosen because Jesus used it when he said, "I am the living water if

you drink of me, you will live." It also means you will be able to go through any challenges that comes your way.

7. This book also gives hope to those who think they have lost it all. You might have been wondering about issues concerning your life. I want you to realize your life is important to the world and our generation. You are created in God's image to accomplish a divine purpose, and that purpose was destined by God before the birth of time . Your future is God's past, and you are intended to walk the path that God has already finished.

8. This book gives you the opportunity to understand some important principles that can change your life and make you a better leader. You will stop pacing frantically, instead you will have a clear focus and be able to contribute to making a difference in this generation and those to come.

9. Finally, I believe that God created the world and all the people in it. People need to discover and know the truth. The truth is the source of freedom. True freedom comes from God, who is the truth. Majority of the ideas contained in this book are taken from God's inspired word, which I believe is the source of all truth. This book has principles and keys that offer the only real truth about leadership and the process of becoming an influential leader in your generation.

Introduction

Education is the most
powerful weapon which
you can use to change the world.
Nelson Mandela

Entebbe to Barcelona via Doha

In October 2015, I was traveling from Entebbe in Uganda to Barcelona in Spain via Doha using Qatar Airways. I was scheduled to attend and participate in a global leader's conference organized by the International Leaders Association.

The airplane took off at 10 p.m. and arrived at Doha International Airport in the early hours of the following day. As the aircraft descended, I was able to enjoy a beautiful view of the entire city and Doha airport. The lights of the city along with the network of roads were magnificent and beautiful, sparkling like diamonds.

As I exited the airplane, I was overwhelmed by the higher than average temperatures which hit me like a blast of furnace compared to the mild temperature of the airplane, and that was entirely different from the cold weather in Entebbe near Lake Victoria. There was a significant difference between the two airports. Entebbe International Airport was so small compared to Hamad International in Doha, with its many runways, infrastructure and capacity. There were an uncountable number of airplanes compared to what I saw in Entebbe.

I waited for a few hours in this beautiful airport before boarding the final leg of my flight to Barcelona, Spain. As I walked around the airport, I was awestruck by the massive investment by the Qatar government to build the new airport. The airport is located in the desert peninsula of the Arab States. Looking around at the area outside the terminal, it was amazing to see how they transformed this arid desert into a high-value capital and business destination. A lot of trading activities were taking place. I enquired about some of the excellent products sold at the airport shops but the prices were too expensive. I realized that I was poor by western standards, yet back home in Uganda, I was privileged more than most of my countrymen and women. I could not afford any of the electronics, but I managed to buy a beautiful book by George Convey.

I finally arrived at Barcelona International Airport about 3 p.m. From there, the drive to Barcelona from the hotel was another 45 minutes. The ride was beautiful. The roads were wide and properly marked, revealing a sense of responsibility among the drivers and the government officials who designed the infrastructure. I checked into Barcelona Four Points Sheraton Hotel at 4 p.m. The hotel room I had booked nearly six months ago was beautiful and extremely organized and neat.

After finishing dinner that evening, I laid down to rest for the first time since I began my nearly 15 hours journey. I reflected on all the things I had witnessed the past day. Remember, I was now in a city that was home to one of the world's best football clubs and where world class players lived and displayed their talents and abilities. For the next week, I was engaged in the conference, listening to different speakers and attending various conferences, workshops, seminars, and side activities.

After each day's activities, I would either walk back to the hotel, board a train or hire a cab. During my visit, I had visited Barcelona Football Club Shopping Complex near the Barcelona Stadium to buy sportswear and shoes for my son George, who loves football. George was selected as his football team captain in their School.

Barcelona is a well organized and planned city with an impressive system of roads and other infrastructure. There seemed to be an effective and accountable government. Taxes are paid, and evading them is impossible. Everything was completely different from what we have in Uganda. As I began preparing for my return trip to Nairobi, some strange thoughts began to haunt me and several questions popped into my head which I could not find easy answers to.

1. Why is the level of organization in Barcelona different from Kampala?
2. Why is Homad International Airport in Qatar a hub for most of the world's airlines?
3. Why do we have a messy road network in Uganda and are unable to expand our airport?
4. Who makes the decisions in Barcelona or Doha for the construction and design of such quality infrastructure?
5. Who should be held accountable for the misery of the people and lack of essential services in my country?
6. What are our leaders doing? Can't they copy what they see happening in other successful countries?

These questions led me to additional thoughts. It was evident that the world is changing at a rate far greater than that of a century or even a decade ago. The book of Daniel prophesied how knowledge would be increased and people would run to and fro, and we are seeing this fulfilled on a daily basis. Every sensible person will need ideas, knowledge, and wisdom that have been tested if they are to successfully navigate in today's world where chaos, confusion and crises have become the order of the day. The 21st Century is going to witness more global wars, conflicts, violence, ideological wars and terrorism than that of previous generations.

To thrive in this world, you will need insight, principles, and wisdom to navigate through life. Without wisdom, the world's challenges will overpower you and destroy your life, community, corporation and nation. Wisdom is more important than wealth and money. You can have money, but without wisdom, you will make wrong decisions and end up heading in the wrong direction or place in your life.

Furthermore, you will need to rise up to become a leader in your own right because you were created by God to be a leader. Our leaders, if not held accountable, will continue to make bad decisions which will impact on future generations. From what I saw in Barcelona or Doha, my simple conclusion is that the beauty and excellence I saw did not happen by accident, they were the result of leaders who guided the planning in areas such as infrastructure, systems, and quality of life. Leaders determine the quality of life of its citizen. However, if the leaders are greedy, selfish, self-centred or oppressive, the citizens will experience everything that comes with bad leadership and governance.

Millions of people have been influenced by their parents, families, friends, associates, and at much higher level by leaders. A leader influences followers through manipulation, coercion, or inspiration. All of us have been and will continue to be influenced by somebody. A person with influence finds a way to dominate, control, direct or affect your decisions, actions, choices, lifestyle, or even your destiny.

An influential person is one whom people respect, obey, listen to, or aspire to be like. An influential person has followers. I remember as a kid; my life was influenced by my father, uncles and other people whom I came to observe over the years. I had to make decisions about who I wanted to positively influence my life.

When you look at people like Nelson Mandela, Jomo Kenyatta, Milton Obote, Kwame Nkrumah, Julius Nyerere, and Abraham Lincoln, one thing they have in common is that they influenced and impacted the generation they lived in. This begs the question; was their influence positive or negative? There are also unknown people who have impacted your community, churches or organizations. Each person has someone who has influenced them, and each person is a leader in some capacity, whether they know it or not.

The Questions of Human Heart and Soul

Every human being is on a journey to discover who they are and make a difference. People are searching for the meaning of life. A lot of discussions and conversations are taking place in the heart of every person. There are 7.5 billion people on Earth at the time of writing this book and every day about 350,000 babies are being born. This means that in the next 50 years, the world population will climax to 9.7 billion.

The question people wrestle with are many.

What Are Those Questions?

1. Who are you?
2. Where did you come from?
3. Where are you going?
4. What can you do with your life?
5. Why are you here on Earth?
6. Do you have a reason for living?

For Leadership, These Questions Are Important:

1. What about my leadership potential?
2. Are you a leader or a follower?
3. Do you have leadership potential?
4. Do you have charisma?
5. Is leadership about charisma?
6. Is leadership about power or possessing wealth?
7. Is leadership about skills, talents, traits or authority?
8. Is leadership about physical appearance?
9. Is leadership a result of family heritage?
10. Are politicians elected to political offices true leaders?
11. What motivates a person to seek a political office?
12. Is leadership a calling?
13. Is leadership about fame or popularity?
14. Is a leader supposed to have followers?
15. Is it a requirement for a leader to have a title?
16. Is leadership for those with wealth?
17. Is leadership the same as management?

Are Leaders The Most Intelligent People in Our World?

Are leaders those individuals who are intelligent, creative, bright, smart, and possess good speaking skills? I struggled with these issues as a youth growing up in the slums in Eastern Uganda. I recall reading books on leadership and related theories at Makerere University. I also encountered lots of leadership principles while studying for my Master's Degree in Organisational Leadership and Management at Uganda Christian University. The course taught me much about the theories and principles of leadership some of which I believe were misleading. I went deeper into the concepts and principles of leadership while studying for doctorate of strategic leadership. This course made matters worse especially the lesson on Leadership Theory. I never agreed with some of the issues that were presented.

Nevertheless, I studied the book *Leadership Theory and Practice* by Peter Northouse. I still could not believe what I was reading and learning. I decided to figure out what Biblical leadership is all about and what leaders do. In this book, you will come to see that true leadership is discovered and manifested.

While studying my Bible during my teenage years, I found a fascinating accounts of people who were leaders. I read about Moses and Joshua who led the Israelites, despite the people's murming and rebellion from Egypt towards the Promised Land. I read about Saul, David, and Solomon and how they conducted themselves as kings of Israel. I read about Peter in the book of Acts, the leader of the community of believers in the early church. I read about Jesus Christ, who led a group of twelve young men from a diverse background of fishermen, tax collectors, doctors and lawyers among others. I read about Joseph, with his brothers and the entire family. I read about Stephen, the first martyr in Acts 6. I read about Nehemiah who motivated and led the people to rebuild the walls of Jerusalem after the city had been destroyed. I read about Esther who risked certain death to lead her people by asking for mercy from a pagan king. What would you call these people? I believe with all my heart they were all godly leaders. They had conviction and an awareness of their purpose in life.

I believe I have been able to discover the answers to the questions that each and every human being struggles to answer. I know you are going to think that Plato, Socrates, and Aristotle are leading experts on leadership and democracy. Yes, these gurus initiated and wrote about issues of their day. They wrote books and sold their ideas about democracy, politics, society, governance, leadership and many others topics. The ideas of all these Greek philosophers continue to influence the way nations or leaders govern and lead, but their views are somehow misleading even today.

Millions of people have been oppressed because of the wrong ideas that Greek philosophers propagated. I believe there is need to correct and write a new message about leadership based on biblical principles. I also think the greatest gift parents can give to their children is the gift of a Bible. Even if you are not a believer in God, give your kids a Bible. Let them read it.

Why Leaders Are Needed?

- Leaders make things happen.
- Leaders cause changes to occur.
- Leaders can destroy or cause development.

- Leaders determines whether or not there will be improvement.
- Leaders determine the development level.
- Leaders are always leading people, families, communities or nations.
- Leaders inspire followers with a vision.
- Leaders take people from the known to the unknown.
- Leaders pursue their vision and purpose.
- Leaders live by their values and principles.

The Challenges Faced by Nations

We read or listen to the news every day about global challenges. We see conflicts in countries like Syria, Iraq, South Sudan, Somalia, Chad, Central Africa Republic, Egypt, and Libya. We see people complain and point fingers at those who have power, guns, and soldiers. People say the leaders are the cause of problems, but are they really the only ones to blame?

I think and believe that the biggest challenge is finding effective leaders who are not manipulators, dictators or oppressors. I believe people in the Eurozone are looking for leaders who can solve the economic problems, as well as the migrant problem. Individuals in the countries listed above are also crying out for true leaders. They are longing for the day when they will not need to worry about a terrorist blowing up their children traveling home on a school bus.

The Leaders Without Leadership

Our world is full of those in leadership, but the saddest thing is many of them are not effective leaders. Effective leaders are concerned with being successful in producing the desired results or intended outcomes. Most of the leaders around the world have manipulate those around them and seek to control them.

There are leaders sitting in parliaments or corporations or organizations. There are leaders in communities. There are leaders in religious groups. There are leaders in both the private and public sector. Each of these leaders must be held accountable for the problems every nation is facing. Every negative event in the world is a result of poor leadership.

The Power of Technology and Culture

When I think about our current generation, what worries other sober-minded individuals and me is the impact technology has on culture and values. Cultures and communities around the world are being eroded like sand on the seas or the oceans. If leaders do not rise and work to restore culture, correct value systems and set high standards of integrity, the world will experience even greater problems than we are witnessing today.

Technological change is occurring at such a rapid pace that life is faster than ever before. People have no time for families because of technology. Young people have no time to read books or engage in meaningful activities because they spend all their time on social media. Marriages are falling apart because young people have not been initiated to traditional values and culture.

Unequal Distribution of Resources and Opportunities

For ages we hear about the haves and have-nots, but despite spending billions on the "war on poverty," the situation remains the same. Poverty is everywhere yet an abundance of resources exist. When I move around the countryside, I never cease to be shocked with how many thousands are living in poverty. Sometime ago, I had the oppourtunity to travel to Kenya and ride with a driver to Kibera, a division of Nairobi Area, and neighborhood of the city of Nairobi. Kibera is the largest slum in Nairobi, and there are many countries with leaders and slums.

If you visit slums in any country, you will observe that majority of the residents live in abject poverty and earn less than a $1 per day. The rates of unemployment are high, and many live with HIV while cases of assault and rape are rapant in this community.

Also, slum has a limited number of schools, and residents there cannot afford quality education for their children. Clean water is scarce, resulting in diseases caused by poor hygiene. A majority of people living in this slum lack access to healthcare and education. I do not want to blame only national leaders but leaders at every level.

When I think about the children in slums, what their future is going to look like, Who will bring them out of poverty, Who will give them the opportunity for better health care and education, Who will liberate them from their current predicament, I became hellbent to write this book.

Understand God's Plan For Creation

A people without the knowledge of their past history, origin and culture is like a tree without roots.

Marcus Garvey

What Was God's Intent of Creation?

There is no reference book that offers God's original intention or plans on creation other than His written Word, The Holy Bible. It remains the only true source of God's mind and information for mankind. In Genesis 1, the author clearly presents everything that happened and how it was carried out. Genesis 1:26-28 gives a clear reason of God's original reason for creating humanity, whom He said should be in His likeness.

In the same way, God created man for a specified assignment. The most important message about Man's assignment is in Genesis 1:26-28. Why would God speak to Adam about ruling the Earth? What does He want man to do? Can you rule the fish? I believe you can catch the fish but not organize them. Can a person rule over everything including wild animals? Can man subdue everything on Earth? These are difficult questions. When Jesus came to Earth and was born of a woman in human flesh, Jesus explained what man was to dominate.

What Is The Culture In The Kingdom Of God?

First, we need to know that heaven is an invisible country where the King, God, sits on the throne. If we all agree that culture is always around us, as the way we live and what we believe, then we can extend the same thinking into understanding heaven's culture. When you ask someone what their culture is, you will hear things like; it is a way of life.

If we are serious about discovering what the culture in heaven looks like, we need to understand the message Jesus spoke about the kingdom of God. The only way you can know what happens at the Palace in the kingdom of Great Britain is to ask the prince or the spokesperson. Jesus Christ, who is Heaven's crown prince told us a lot about the kingdom of God in Heaven.

The Bible is considered a religious book by millions of people. To me, the Bible is God's message about Himself as a King, His sons, and dominion. Genesis 1 gives the story of creation. Genesis 2 gives the detailed account of God's creative works and where God put the first man in garden and said, *"you are free to eat everything in the Garden, but never eat fruit from one particular tree, for the day you do, you will die spiritually."* Genesis 3 records the fall of man from dominion or kingship over all of creation and the subsequent punishment for disobedience. Then the story continues in Genesis 4 where we learn about the consequences of sin and how it corrupted the entire human race as we read about two brothers,

Cain and Abel. By that time God was no longer in fellowship with man the way he was in the garden.

Let's look at what Jesus told his followers. *"From that time on Jesus began to preach, 'Repent, for the kingdom of heaven has come near'"* (Matthew 4:17). Imagine hearing that sermon. Why repent? Because man lost dominion over the Earth in Genesis 3, and Jesus came to restore that relationship. God had disconnected Himself from man, who had become a fugitive and was out of fellowship with God.

Next, in Matthew 4:23, we read; *"Jesus went throughout Galilee, teaching in their synagogues, proclaiming the good news of the kingdom, and healing every disease and sickness among the people."* Again, he proclaimed the good news of the kingdom. What is this kingdom thing? What was Jesus talking about? *"Blessed are the poor in spirit, for theirs is the kingdom of heaven"* (Matthew 5:3). Imagine how the people living in poverty during his day must have reacted on hearing the good news that they would one day take ownership of God's kingdom of heaven.

Furthermore, Matthew 6:9-10 reads: *"This, then, is how you should pray: 'Our Father in heaven, hallowed be your name, your kingdom come, your will be done, on Earth as it is in heaven."* Can you think about the above statement? Jesus is teaching the disciples how they should pray. He is saying the Kingdom of His Father has come to Earth. He also says we should let the will of His Father be done on Earth as it is done in Heaven.

"But seek first his kingdom and his righteousness, and all these things will be given to you as well" (Matthew 6:33). Here he tells

the disciples what should be their top priority which is seeking first His Kingdom and his righteousness, and then everything they wanted would be given.

If you are right in the sight of the king, you will enjoy the benefits of being a citizen of that kingdom. Righteousness is about the right relationship with the king. The opposite is also true. Jesus said; your priority should be to seek the kingdom. Seeking means that what is sought does not come easily. You have to do all you can to find the kingdom and king. Seeking is searching with vigor, determination and looking everywhere to get it.

Is that what the church is teaching Christians? The message most pastors, bishops or church leaders preach on a Sunday morning is that of grace, salvation, blessings, and love, while ignoring the message of the kingdom of God. Do leaders know what the top priority is? What is your priority in life as a leader?

Matthew 9:35 says, *"Jesus went through all the towns and villages, teaching in their synagogues, proclaiming the good news of the kingdom and healing every disease and sickness."* That same message is still being repeated and proclaimed. He also healed those who were sick and had diseases. Jesus went to every town and village to proclaim the good news of the kingdom. What is the good news? Taking back what was lost during the Fall of Man in the Garden of Eden. Matthew 10:7-8 says, *"As you go, proclaim this message: 'The kingdom of heaven has come near.' Heal the sick, raise the dead, cleanse those who have leprosy, drive out demons. Freely you have received; freely give."*

Why Did Jesus Use The Word "This Message"?

As a results of man's fallen nature, Jesus knew that if he did not make it clear whose message they were to deliver, they would change it and create their own message. Some people can misinterpret messages and to avoid this, the leader must be clear and specific. The message was about the kingdom. He never told the disciples to preach about how they survived the storm in the Sea of Galilee, or how they fed 4,000. He never wanted the preachers to talk about how he healed the sick, the blind or lame, or delivered demon-posssessed men, but to preach or proclaim the message about the kingdom. But if you are delivered out of the hands of demons by the Spirit of God, the Kingdom of God has come upon you (Matthew 12:28).

He replied, *"The knowledge of the secrets of the kingdom of heaven has been revealed or given to you, but not to them"* (Matthew 13:11).

Notice that knowledge of the secrets of the kingdom of heaven were only revealed to those who listened to him. The word secret, as used by Jesus, implies laws or principles. A leader who does not live according to laws or principles will be a failure. Most leaders today are more interested in power than principles.

Jesus Used Parables to Teach Followers

Have you ever read the paarables that Jesus taught the disciples? In one of His message, see what He said: *Listen to what the parable of the sower means; When anyone hears the message about the kingdom and does not understand it, the evil one comes and snatches away... was sown in his heart* (Matthew 13:18-19).

Another parable He spoke to them: *"The kingdom of heaven is like leaven, which a woman took and hid in three measures of meal till it was all leavened.* (Matthew 13:33).

The New Internationa Version of the Bible presents it as, *"He told them still another parable: 'The kingdom of heaven is like yeast that a woman took and mixed into about sixty pounds of flour until it worked all through the dough.'"*

Leaders must learn to use parables to teach, their followers. The great leader used parables to share His mesgage. It is one of the most effective ways to teach followers. What approach do you apply in teaching your followers?

Experience of Mixing Yeast and Dough at Choices Bread Bakery

In 2013, I invested about $40,000 to open a bakery for unemployed university graduates in Kampala. The bakery produced different kind of bread like brown bread, white bread, pancakes and other products. The purchasing officer had to buy all the ingredients. When all the ingredients were mixed with flour without yeast, the final product will not be bread. But when yeast is added, it will work out and influence the dough.

When the bread is placed into the oven, it expand in size. The yeast makes the bread grow. In other words, it influences the bread. In the parable above, Jesus was saying when you receive the kingdom, you will work it out. You will influence your neighborhood. You have influence just like the yeast.

The statement in Matthew 13:33 is about influence, dominion and impact . Leaders must have influence, dominion and impact with their followers. Matthew 16:19 makes it even more interesting by quoting what Jesus said *"I will give you the keys of the kingdom of heaven; whatever you bind on Earth will be bound in heaven, and whatever you loose on Earth will be loosed in heaven."*

"And this gospel of the kingdom will be preached in the whole world as a testimony to all nations, and then the end will come" (Matthew 24:14). The phrase world has a different meaning in Hebrew. It means systems. Jesus said, when the kingdom message had been preached to all systems in the Earth only then will the end come.

The writer of Hebrews 12:6 says, *"It is impossible to please God without faith."* How can you please God? Do you please God by giving gifts in the church? Do you please God by offering or paying your tithe? God is never pleased by those things unless they are accompanied by faith. God is a king. A king is excited when His people or subjects obey, respect and have faith in Him. As for God, the only thing that makes God pleased is faith. When a citizen has faith in a king, everything they need will be received.

Faith is a condition for enjoying the benefits in a kingdom. Without confidence in the king, it is impossible to enjoy the free gifts from the king. A king does not seek permission from parliament or councils on how to or whom to give the wealth. A king gives wealth to those who are faithful. A king does not submit a budget for discussion. A king's word is final. The words of a king are law. When a king speaks, His word is law. When you study those passages carefully, you will realize that Jesus talked about faith because everything was about the kingdom. Whose kingdom? The kingdom of God. How do things get done in the kingdom of God?

"Then He touched their eyes and said, *'According to your faith let it be done to you"* (Matthew 9:29). If you will remember what we said about culture, it is the way people do things or a way of life. You can also see the kingdom of God; things get done using faith. The text in Matthew says, *according to your faith it shall be done to you.* Faith, therefore, is a cultural charateristic in the kingdom of heaven. You cannot do business with God unless you have faith. God cannot do anything with you unless He is assured that you believe in him. Jesus said; *"Whoever believes in me will have eternal life."*

John 3:16 says, *"For God so loved the world, that he gave His only Son, that whoever believes in him, will not perish but have everlasting life."* The word "believes" is the root word from "belief". Belief means faith. If you believe something, it means you have faith in it.

One day Jesus asked his disciples, *"When the Son of Man comes will He find faith on Earth?"* (Luke 18:8b). What an interesting question. To me, this means that the kingdom of heaven is full of faith. Jesus is not looking for your culture; his interest is faith or belief. Jesus was not concerned about your power, wealth, houses, property, he is interested in your faith.

Put another way, in the country where I live, a poor person is one who has no money or currency. When you have money, you can buy property, houses, land or even bribe voters to get elected. Some of our leaders have bought their way to power. Can you imagine buying off the electorate to become a leader? To me, that is not true leadership. I recall meeting one of the politicians in my country at Standard Chartered Bank, exchanging bank notes to get coins he was going to distribute to voters for political support (buying votters." I asked the "leader" what he was doing; and he said that he was going to "repair the classroom of a primary school." But to me I knew, he was not honest.

There are many similar stories of some leaders accused of bribing their voters, and some have been kicked out of parliament for bribery. To me, only a small portion of leaders are genuine while the majority are engaged in illegal activities, and they will not escape the punishment of God. If they are to escape divine punishment, they ought to repent and ask God for forgiveness.

When acted upon, faith gets things done. In the kingdom of God, faith is the currency. Jesus said, *"If you have faith as small as a mustard seed, then you can tell the mountain to move and it will obey."*

The Concept of the Kingdom of Heaven

In Uganda, we have different kingdoms that historically have their own territories. These kingdoms are: Buganda Kingdom, Toro Kingdom, Bunyoro Kingdom, Rwenzururu Kingdom and others. I have had an opportunity to visit all those places and interact with the people there. In 2010, I had a chance to visit the palace of the Tooro Kingdom when working with UNICEF Uganda. The Tooro Kingdom covers the districts of Kabarole, Kamwenge, Kyenjojo, Kyaka, and Kyegegwa. King Oyo was celebrating the anniversary of ascending to the throne. I learned that a kingdom has a territory which is dominated by a king and the subjects obey the king.

A king is more important and powerful than a President, Member of Parliament, Chief, Counselor or a Mayor. A king owns the territory and gives the land to his citizens or subjects. When a national anthem is being sung, the king does not normally stand up, but the president has to stand up to respect the national anthem. I believe a lot of people, including many Christians, have very limited knowledge of kingdoms.

What Jesus mean when He said *"The kingdom of God has arrived"*. He meant that a country where God lives has come to Earth. This means the kingdom of heaven is not a religion. Jesus did not say, "Christianity has arrived." He said the kingdom has come. Jesus did not come to bring Christianity or a religious organization. His message was about the kingdom of heaven, not Christianity or religion. The message of Jesus Christ was about the Kingdom of God coming to the Earth, just as it is in Heaven.

The Current State of Human Beings in the World

The lack of influence and effective leadership has made millions of people powerless, hopeless, faithless and defenseless. People have lost confidence, and their perspective of life has completely broken down.

People are Suffering Because of Any of the Following:

1. Fear

People fear terrorists, ethnic violence, tribal clashes, natural disasters, epidemics, unemployment, the collapse of state authority and political conflicts. I was in Garowe, Somalia when a suicide bomber killed humanitarian workers on 20 April 2015 who were providing immunization programs for children.

2. Lost Hope and Faith

People are perplexed, disillusioned, and have lost hope in life. A young lady who was a student of the University of Nairobi told me she had lost hope of getting a job because her brothers and sisters still have no jobs five years after graduation. Older people are wondering what will happen when they retire.

3. Anger

The majority of the people are not happy. People are frustrated with life and are unable to deal with the daily challenges. Men are beating their wives and women are losing the patience in their marriages. Marriages are collapsing at a rate faster than expected. Young people are unhappy with the parents who are absent from home, and they carry this bitterness into their community.

4. Mistrust and Distrust

There is no longer trust among people. People no longer keep their promises. A leader's words or promises cannot be trusted. Voters are demanding payment before voting because when politicians are elected they are expected to earn more and voters are forgotten until the next elections. The schools and universities do a poor job preparing students to face the challenges in the world.

5. Spirit of Compromise

There is no longer regard or respect for values, let alone morals. People have learned to compromise and accept things as just being part of life. Bosses and subordinates are in relationships for the sake of job security and to obtain promotions. Students are sleeping with their lecturers to get good grades and earn a degree.

6. Selfishness

The spirit of sharing has eroded like sand in the ocean. People are thinking about themselves and are self-centred or family centered. Politicians extend the term of parliament from five years to seven because its of benefit to them . We have greed in every community, church and parliaments. Leaders have become so selfish and greedy.

7. Competitive Attitudes

People have become so obsessed with success and competition that they frequently compete for resources, wealth, and power. Even family members are fighting each other. Competition should not be taken at the expense of collaboration and cooperation and partnerships.

8. Greed

People are greedier than ever before. People are materialistic. People begin to crave for goods that they are unable to get in an ethical manner. Young ladies are busy running after men who have money. They want to succeed faster and not willing to go through the process. Young people are borrowing loans from commercial banks and institutions to buy cars they cannot afford to service and maintain.

9. Life Has Lost Value

Human life no longer has value. Young ladies are aborting babies, and this is considered normal. In every country, there are popular places where young women and older ones sell their bodies in exchange for money.

10. Abuse

Parents and guardians are abusing the rights of children. There is constant domestic violence. Husbands beat their wives or even kill them. Wives plan to kill their spouse in the name of getting wealth or inheriting wealth.

11. Violence and Conflict

The world is witnessing the vicious cycle of violence. There is violence in parts of the world and countries such as: South Sudan, Somalia, Mali, Chad, Central African Republic, Nigeria, Libya, and Syria. The world is experiencing wars today on a higher scale as never seen before . There is an ideological war. There is religious wars. There are political wars. There are tribal or ethnic wars. There are business wars. There is even an internal war in church among the clergy.

Why do Leaders Fail in their Responsibilities?

1. Faithlessness

Our leaders today have no faith in God. The leaders are faithless. They believe in their wealth and money, or in the power of a gun. When they do think on spiritual things, they believe in witchcraft.

2. Polygamy and Adultery

Everywhere you go, you find men in polygamous relationships. People have rented houses for spouses, and are engaged in illicit relationships. Leaders are supposed to be exemplary, but that is now considered old-fashioned. Pastors are being caught having affairs with church members. Politicians are having affairs with secretaries, and bosses are having sexual relationships with their employees.

3. Lack of Self-discipline and Self-control

Our leaders lack discipline and self-control. They have lost all pretense of values and morality. The standards for life have been compromised. Leaders lack self-control and like to enjoy the freedom to do as they please.

4. Drunkenness

Our leaders spend time in bars and lodges rather than being at home with their spouses and children. The leaders are busy drinking and spending all their income in bars. When they manage to go back home, they are unable to meet their domestic needs and responsibilities. The source of domestic violence is the inability to meet basic needs for the family.

5. Bad Behaviour

It has been said, what you see is what you get. Bad parents are an example to their children. Children, who are the future leaders, also become drunkards, and this makes them behave in a bad way. Bad company corrupts good character and morals.

6. Greed

Our leaders today think of their stomachs or privileges (Romans 16:18). Today's leaders think about themselves, regardless of the cost to future generations. The attitude of "everyone for him or herself and God for us all" has overtaken the world.

7. Lack of Integrity and Honesty

Integrity is when you are true to yourself and accountable and responsible. Our leaders are shameless. They lack integrity, engaging in bad habits; corruption among others. The love for money is too much for them to handle.

8. Leaders Fuel Conflict

Sometimes the source of conflict is our leaders. Their pride has gone above their heads and controls all they do. Our leaders never listen to followers, even when the advice is sound. Our l eaders are arrogant and irresponsible.

9. Wrong Associations

Some of our leaders rely on bad advisors. They never have time or the desire to seek out the truth if it might offend them. Whatever is given to them by personal assistants is considered correct, so long as the advisors are "yes" men. In some cases, information is hidden from the leaders.

10. Ego Problems

There are some leaders who believe they are above being advised. They feel they know everything. The truth is nobody knows everything. Remember only God knows everything.

The Role of Leadership and Business Schools

There are thousands and hundreds of business and leadership schools that train leaders in our world today. I have noticed that the majority of those who go to leadership schools end up becoming managers, administrators and hold high offices or title. They are leaders, but sometimes they control, manipulate or manage people rather than lead. In my country, we have a National Leadership Institute where our political elites enrol for "leadership training or development." Sometimes I wonder what happens when they come back; they learn about management of people but this is not necessarily leadership. I believe they learn techniques of controlling and manipulating people. Only a few demonstrate true leadership.

The Need for Mind Renewal of our Leaders

I believe change is possible. Romans 12: 2 says, *"Do not be conformed to the patterns of this world, but be transformed by the renewal of your minds."* Paul was telling the early church that the most important thing people or leaders need to change is the way they think. Renewal of the mind means changing how we think. There is a need to modify the bank of our thoughts and receive new insights and fresh ideas. When you change what you think, you become different. If do not change the way you think, your life and future are at risk; and is likely going to get worse. The right action for initiating change is an admission of the need for change. There must be acceptance. One of the things that destroys people is pride. Millions are in "hell" today because of pride.

The Change Process

I believe that change takes place when there is conception. What do I mean by conception? In this case, it means "the action of conceiving a child or of a child being conceived." When a man and a woman are in a relationship, they can be in it, but a change in the woman occurs when the woman gets pregnant. Therefore, if you want to change, you must conceive. If you have been doing bad things or have a bad habit, you can decide to change by conceiving.

Change also happens when there is a fight to keep the new ideas. I like what Paul told Timothy. He said; *"Fight the good fight of faith"* (I Timothy 6:12a). Sometimes the devil makes you think you are not saved or born again. Challenges of life might make you doubt, or lose faith in God, but Paul says; *"Fight a good fight of faith."* This means that you have to fight to keep your beliefs, otherwise you will lose it or give up.

The Mentoring and Coaching Gap

If the nations, communities, and societies want to get true leaders, there must be efforts made in the area of mentoring and coaching. A mentor grooms people to become like him over a given period through teaching, observation and giving assignments. It is a tragedy for families to lack successors when the parents die. It is a tragedy for good leaders not to pass their knowledge and wealth of experiences on to the next generation.

KNOW
THAT EVERY PERSON
CAN LEAD

Understand The Power Of A Seed

*God has equipped you to handle difficult things.
In fact, He has already planted the seeds of discipline
and self-control inside you. You just have to water
those seeds with His Word to make them grow.*
Joyce Meyer

The Power of a Seed "The Seed Principle"

When I was young, my grandparents were peasants farmers involved in subsistence agriculture. Subsistence farming is a type of farming where everything that is produced is sold. Subsistence farming is not commercial farming or producing for the market. Every season they had to plant food. My parents had to use their own instincts regarding the rainfall pattern. There was no rain gauge or weather station to predict the weather. Our work as kids was to support them by working in the garden.

I recall as a child, the four of us were given a basin of groundnuts to plant in the garden. which was about an acre. We had to prepare the garden before planting the seeds. The garden was divided into four parts with each child given a portion to plant. It looked tiresome and was an appalling task. I came to hate agricultural work.

However, when I grew up, I learned lessons that have changed and shaped my life. The two critical lessons that have continued to influence my life until this present day are:

1. Every seed has a tree, fruit, more seeds and trees. So it is with anyone.
2. The future of a seed is inside itself. Your future is not ahead of you, but within you. It is your choices and decisions determine your destiny.

The Process of Seed Multiplication

There are no other ways that seeds can be multiplied or increased unless something has been done. As a matter of fact, if a seed is to be multiplied or increased there are certain processes to be followed. These processes are described here:

1. Preparation

This is the first step in undertaking agricultural work. I recall during the dry season; we had to clear the bush and remove all the thorns in the garden before plowing. If we didn't, they would sprout back up and choke out the seeds we were going to plant. Preparation also involved getting the right seeds for the garden. It would do us no good to plant orange seeds because there was not enough water.

With life's many challenges, preparation is an important aspect of life. It has been said greatness is not in the performance, it is in the preparation. Behind every great athlete, doctor, actor, or anyone who is well-respected in their field are untold hours of training and learning. It did not just come to them overnight. If you are going to change the world and impact your generation, you must spend time preparing. Without preparation, you are setting yourself up for failure.

Preparation is analogous to a person who wants to take a trip to a foreign country. Long before he arrives there, the person begins by getting information about the country, where he or she will stay, what he will do once there, local customs, etc. Preparation involves paying for a ticket. Preparation is the process of examining the road map to the desired destination. Without preparation, success will be haphazard and if you happen to have a successful trip it will be due more to happenstance.

2. Planting

The next phase before a harvest is planting. This is where the seeds are sowed and covered with dirt so they can grow. Planting can be done in straight lines or just strewn at random. The farmer places the right seeds in the garden at the right depth so they can germinate. Planting should not be done when there is too much rain or sunshine. In life, planting is equivalent to taking the time to think and reflect on what you hope to acomplish. It is a time to write down your visions and goals. It also involves throwing away wrong or bad seeds. A farmer that wants to get a great harvest will plant as many quality seeds as possible.

Taking the time to plant means that you sacrifice some of the things you have in order to produce more. It could involve paying money to obtain a second degree. It might have been that you studied courses which you had no interest in. It could also mean stopping some of the relationships you have been involved in that made you lose sight of your vision and stopped you from dreaming or exploiting your gifts, talents and potential. It has been said, "A person without dreams is a poor person." Likewise, a person whose vision does not materialize is a frustrated person. People without vision has idle potentials.

The germination process occurs when the seeds have been covered and buried with soil and are given water and oxygen. My science teachers in primary seven taught us three conditions necessary for germination and includes: water, soil, and oxygen. Germination is a time when the seed is isolated from other seeds. It is this particular moment when the seed begins to manifest its real ability and a time to start the journey to its intended destination.

Every human who wishes to influence the world must go through this process.

In order to germinate and bring forth new life, the seed must die. Germination means dying to old associations and friendships that are not contributing towards the desired destination. Germination might also mean to cut off some habits, practices, bad activities and motives. Germination is important because it is a phase of change and transformation. As you take steps towards your desired goals, check and determine your germination ability, rate, and state.

3. Weeding

When the seeds begin to grow, there is something else that wants to grow beside them. The next activity is weeding the garden. For those of you who are familiar with agriculture or subsistence farming, you know how hard and tedious this can be. It seems like a never-ending job. Weeding is the process of separating good/wanted plants from harmful plants. There are some people you might have grown up with you or studied with you who are weeds in your life. They will attempt to choke out the good fruits you are trying to bear. They are competing with your good seeds for food, nutrients or water. As a leader, you need to identify the weeds and separate them from the group, organization or team.

4. Maturity

This is the phase when the fruits are given time to mature. Take the example of corn or maize. When the corn first appears,it is tiny and referred to as "baby corn." For most uses, you need to allow the maize to grow so you can prepare it for harvest. Maturity is the phase when you are now responsible and accountable for your actions and decisions. However, not all adults are mentally and spiritually mature. I have met people who are 40, 50, 60 or 70 years old and still behave like children or teenagers. These people still engage in things like attending night clubs or trans night parties or celebrations. They have not matured to a point where some of their youthful engagements are no longer right for them.

5. Harvesting

This is the last activity farmers do until the next season. I recall we planted groundnuts, but during harvest, we could roast them while in the garden or at home. Harvest period is when the farmer gets to enjoy the fruits of their sweat and labor. But this does not mean he focuses on the present alone at the detriments of the future. Harvest period is also when fruits are stored for the winter and seeds are set aside for the next season. What will people harvest from your life? You need to apply these concepts to your own life. Just as a seed goes through a process to produce a tree and fruits, you too can become a leader. The processes include; preparation, planning, weeding, maturing and harvesting.

Primary School Lessons Learned from the Seed Principle

I believe there are many lessons, but this lesson is about life and your influence. I learned that when you plant a basket of groundnuts, care for them properly and weed out the bad plants; you will harvest a lot of seeds. I recall us planting four basins which are like 40 kilograms of groundnuts, but during the harvest; the return on our yield was over two granaries that could store up to 30 bags during the bumper harvest. We could plant a few kilograms which might result to plenty during harvest .

I recall in Primary four, there were lessons in math which involved the conversion of meters to centimeters, decimetres, and grams to kilograms. The teacher was a tough man who would not tolerate those who failed to convert or carry out simple arithmetic, so I had to learn the units if I was to escape his punishment. Also, during science lessons, there was a lesson of putting bean seeds into ground and cover it with soil. Then it would become a plant. At home, our grandmother used to take us early morning to dig. I hated it just as many people hate work. I learned and discovered that when you plant, you will harvest more than you planted in most cases. I believe life is this way.

Another lesson is when the weeds are left to compete with plants, they will usually win the battle, resulting in a poor harvest. Life is also that way. If you do not uproot the weeds in your life, you will always have a poor harvest. There are people in your life that you have been living with for years who are just like weeds. They need to be removed if you are ever going to get a great output.

To harvest, you must prepare, plant and weed and allow growth. One thing that I have to share with you honestly is that leaders can be developed, but it takes hard work to harvest them. If you want to be great you can, but it's a personal choice. Everything in life is about personal choices. You can choose to watch movies the whole day rather then read and study. You can decide to go clubbing from Friday to Sunday or you can go to church. You can pray or you can sleep the whole day. You can go to work, or you can call off so you can go for holidays on the beach. You can go back to school or college. You can do anything you want. It is a personal choice. But if you are tired of what is happening in your life, then you have to make the right decisions and take personal responsibility.

Be willing to go through the process or stages from preparation to harvest.

What Must You Do?

You need to discover something you want to plant. Planting might mean going back to obtain a college degree or certificate. Planting might mean starting a business. Planting might mean changing a career. Planning is like investing. When you invest in a project, you will gain revenue or profits but only if you do all the other things. Think about your life! Where do you want to go? Your life is like a seed, which if planted and allowed to germinate, will produce fruits that will be harvested. Fruits are what makes you impactful and influential. Do you have a fruit to serve?

Gift to Newborn in our Teso Culture

In my culture, like many other cultures, when a baby is born, parents, aunties, uncles, grandparents and family friends will bring unique gifts to the child. During Jesus' birth, the "wise men from the East" brought gifts to offer for Him. I am the firstborn among my father's children, and I received gifts. When I began to understand, I was told that my uncle gave me a cow as a gift. By the time I was seven I had three cows, and by the time I was 14, I had over 14 cows. I asked myself how could one cow multiply and produce so many cows?

During those years, I used to graze the cows, and it was interesting to look after them and see their response. If you are raised in a farming community, you know the feeling I am talking about. But my wealth was taken away when cattle raids occurred in our region. I will never forget how within one day, all our cows were stolen and we were left with nothing.

However, I learned a lesson that I will never forget. Every cow has the potential to produce and give us gifts such as milk, cheese, and other products. As a human being, you must understand that you have to use your gifts and serve the world. The world is waiting for you to deliver the gifts that are in you. It is the gift that makes you powerful and influentual. Why is Christiano Ronaldo or Lionel Messi known all over the world? These two are not highly educated, but they have the gift of playing football. This is not something they bought from school, but instead, they were born with those gifts; and they cannot be taken away. Only failure to develop and practice will cause the gift to die. If you deliver your gift to people, it will make people believe in you and you make an impact in your generation. Your gift will bring you before great men and women. Do you have a hidden gift?

Nwanko Kanu, Football Legend from Nigeria

I was in Lagos some years back, and I saw a hospital built by a former footballer, Nwankwo Kanu. This legendary footballer had little education, but used his gift to play for the national team of Nigeria, the *Super Eagles*, as well as big clubs in English football. He was born with his gift. He grew with his gift. He identified, developed and refinded his natutal gift. The gift took him to places that I believe some of the highly educated people in Nigeria and other parts of the world might never visit. His gift exposed him and brought him before great men and women. He used the fruits of his seed to build a hospital for people suffering from heart-related diseases. Kanu's gift has made him impactful. His name will never be erased.

What is your gift?

The True Concepts About Leadership

Researchers, scholars, and speakers have said much about leadership. One of the famous gurus who has written on the theories of leadership is Dr. Peter Northouse. However, through research and study of the scriptures, I am convinced that everyone is a leader, and we all have the power to dominate, govern and rule or subdue. God said in Genesis 1:26; *"Let us make man in our image, after our likeness..."* Nowhere is it written that some are intended to lead while others are created to follow. Every person is both a leader and a follower in some capacity, but the potential for leadership must be fed, developed, discovered, cultivated and learned.

Mother Teresa was a primary teacher in one of the schools in India. One day she decided to serve the poor people who were all over the streets of Calcutta. Her gift was to serve the poor, and she excelled at it. She became a world famous, sought-after leader, and onetime, she addressed the United Nations General Assembly. I recall one of the athletes in Uganda in 2009, Moses Kipsiro, who became influential because he won an Olympic gold medal. Every person who has a gift and decides to use that gift to serve will influence those around him or her.

Leadership is directing, guiding and influencing followers to pursue goals for the benefit of the group. Leadership is the capacity to influence others through inspiration, motivated by passion, generated by the vision and determined by a sense of destiny to achieve a desired purpose.

It must be noted there is likely no human being who does not love power and leadership. People are just afraid to lead or use power. A majority of people love power and want more of it. They also love being in charge. However, people without power are powerless. In fact, powerlessness means you have little or no power. Powerlessness emanates from oppressions by opressors. The oppressor makes you think you are powerless and unimportant. The oppressors like to hide knowledge from the oppressed. Oppresors make people inferior because permission is given by the oppressed. It must be noted that when oppressors are allowed to oppress, nothing will be changed. In short, what you allow, you can't change. For you to change something, you need to confront or face it.

Now What is True Leadership?

There are many defintions of leadership that have been given and shared in world literature. All those definitions are good, but ideas evolve and time changes everything. Based on personal reflection and studies on the nature of leadership and leaders. I have the following to offer as to what I feel real leadership is all about.

1. *Leadership is the emergence of individuals who take up the responsibility to change circumstances and situations and work to make a world a better place.*

2. *Leadership is simply taking up responsibilities to guide groups of people or followers who are seeking guidance to achieve a common goal.*

3. *Leadership is influencing followers to achieve certain ends to change the present circumstances in favor of a preferred future.*

4. *Leadership is the pursuit of vision and purpose for a better world.*

Who Made the Following People Leaders?

Mother Teresa

It's might be hard to know because she has already gone to be with the Lord. However, I am convinced that she became a leader because of the decision she made. She had her gift, which she chose to use to serve people, and they responded to this and decided to follow her. People will follow you when you serve your gift to them. If you want to be great, become a servant. Greatness comes from service, not power. Power is something that has affected relationships and destroyed families, communities, and states.

Are you in charge of your destiny?

Everyone has a gift and has the potential to serve. Even in the famous American Military Academy, West Point, they understand this concept. Those who are being trained to be the future generals spend their first years there as servants having to do menial tasks such as cleaning a toilet with a toothbrush or shining the shoes of upper classmen. This is because America understands the way to produce the best leaders is to make sure they understand they are a servant to those they lead.

Nelson Mandela

Nelson Mandela was a young black man who went to school like anyone else. His dream was to serve as a lawyer. He went to London to study law. After completing his studies, Mandela returned to his native South Africa where he witnessed the oppression of his people through a system known as "Apartheid."

Apartheid was implemented to ensure the South African black people were oppressed by the minority white population. This oppression led Mandela to fight for freedom. He was locked up in jail, but he never gave up. He saw injustice and wanted every South African to have the same rights. It was this fighting for freedom that made him a leader. When you fight for something with a good attitude and right motives, people will follow you, and you will lead them because they want you to lead them. True leaders fight for the good cause. True leaders fight against injustice. True leaders are willing to give up everything for the greater good of people.

Do you see some similarities in the lives of Nelson Mandela and Mother Teresa? They sacrificed everything for everyone. They became leaders who will not be forgotten by history. To them, history was more important than money and wealth. How do you see your leaders today? Do you associate their names with corruption? If so, those are not real leaders; they are corrupt leaders and manipulators.

3

Why People Never Become Leaders

Leaders think and talk about the solutions.
Followers think and talk about the problems.
Brian Tracy

Why do People Fail to Become Leaders?

There are many reasons why people never become leaders. In this section, I will give you a few of them and after I will request that you do further reseach to establish other contributing factors.

1. Adoption of Greek Leadership Theories

I have been involved in leadership studies that have lasted about 15 years. I have had the previledge to study most of the leadership theories taught in colleges and universities. The ideas advanced by people such as Plato, Socrates, and Aristotle among others have also influenced millions of people on the concept of leadership. These Greek thinkers did a great job in sharing their thoughts and ideas to the world, and their ideas have continued to influence and shape our culture to this day. Some of their ideas were good and right, but others are dangerous, misleading and wrong. The reason the 20th Century experienced two bloody world wars can also be linked to bad ideas and philosophies that were propagated and spread by leaders who used those ideas to manipulate, control or govern society.

For instance, Hitler used his inspiring oratory skills to fulfill a need felt by Germans that they were wronged by the terms of the Treaty of Versailles that ended World War 1 and were being unfairly punished. He used these feelings to oppress many people which led to the killings of over six million Jews. Hitler is an example of a leader who used wrong ideas to destroy millions of people in the world. His ideas were more similar to the Greek ideas on leadership that were misleading and inccorect. The Greek ideas contradict God's word in the Bible.

2. The Negative Influence of Culture

One of the most dangerous things in the world is culture and tradition. Tradition is what is passed down from one generation to another, and it occurs through believing culture to the extent that it becomes real. The culture we find ourselves in can be a good motivator on one side and, at the same time, be a bad motivator. Culture can destroy but also build, depending on how you take and use it. Most of the people I have met have resisted change. When change is introduced or proposed, they would say, "But this is how we have always done it, and so it shall be forever."

Culture does not allow deviation from the status quo. In Uganda, one of the tribes has a king who is supposed to be respected by lying down in front of him. Anyone who does what is contrary to established norms is regarded as disrespectful to the king and culture.

Every culture has a way in which it devalues human beings, producing pressure to believe in the culture. In a culture where drinking alcohol is the norm, many people become vagabonds and idiots. Some people I knew from the university who were top students ended up being drunkards. I recall watching a promising leader and a university graduate of zoology and botany destroy his life through alcohol.

Another student filled with potential was discontinued from pursuing a bachelor's degree at Makerere University. Rather than focus on their education and pursuing their dreams, they gave their life to drinking alcohol and every day their lives were getting worse. They would often tell me to join them in the drinking pubs because this was our culture. I did not join their group because I realized if culture causes people to abandon their careers, education or studies, then that culture is not healthy. Culture is a good thing if it teaches morals and character. On the other hand, culture is bad when it leads to the destruction of the leader that is trapped inside of every person.

I often lived with my uncle during holidays in Mukono, Uganda. There was a bar where people would come to drink every evening and on weekends. They would spend hundreds of Ugandan shillings buying beer, gin, and brew. They would also buy roasted pork and fish. I watched several of the customers whose lives were wasted as a result of alcohol consumption and cigarette smoking show up at my uncle's home. I was invited or asked to drink with them, and I would politely refuse. I looked at the lifestyle of those people and said to myself that if I start drinking my life will end up in the same way and my dreams would never be achieved. If I had followed my culture, my dreams and leadership potential would have been buried.

3. The Brainwashing Effect

To be brainwashed means your brain is replaced by another person's thoughts and ideas, and you have no control over your actions and your thoughts seem to have no meaning. I read an article in 2001, immediately after September 11, on how terrorist leaders recruit young people into their group. The report said they are taught to believe terrorism is the best way of life and when you kill an infidel, you will go to *Aljanna* (heaven) and get 72 virgins.

When children are taught something over and over again, they end up believing one side of the story or message. In the early years of the National Resistance Movement, the political party that has ruled Uganda since 1986 came to power and introduced political education, there was a common word that was spoken, "siasa," a Kiswahili word for "brainwashing."

Brainwashing is the saddest thing if it happens to anyone. A person who lacks knowledge is easy to brainwash because they are easily impressionable. The greatest enemy of man is ignorance, not the devil or Satan. An ignorant person is easy to manipulate and oppress. The way to reduce the impact of culture and the effect of brainwashing is to recognize your need for knowledge. When you learn about something, you will not be brainwashed easily. Brainwashing is fought by getting awareness and understanding and applying wisdom. Going back to the statement that you are a leader in your own right, I want you to know that your culture has taught you that only some people are leaders and all others are followers. You have been brainwashed to the point that you do not believe in yourself.

A lion has a leadership spirit as well as an attitude greater than all other animals in the jungle. You must be willing to go through training if you are to lead and be an influence. Young lions become leaders because they participate and learn from the lioness. If you want to learn leadership, you must be willing to join the training. When the cubs are born, they always stay with their mother. The lioness will care for the young cubs and train them on important aspects of jungle life. Jungle life is tough and only the tough will survive. Young cubs grow to master the game and dominate the jungle environment. The same applies to you and me; we need an attitude and the spirit of leadership.

4. Bad Environments, Associations and Groups

Every time people think or talk about environment, most think about trees and forests or the ecosystem. In this context, I want to narrow it down to where you live. Most of our beliefs come from our interaction with our family. Parents teach their children what they know and have learned. I am a parent, and I look after my family and relatives. I show my family and relatives what I believe is correct and right. I also warn them of dangers. Parents teach their families their ideas, culture, philosophy and theology. If these ideas are wrong, it affects their aptitude and altitude in life.

Parents who always tell their children they are useless because of a slight mistake are destroying them. The children will end up believing what the parents say is true, and think to themselves, "Why even try." The message then gets stored in the brain and affects their attitudes and actions.

A healthy environment is one where positive ideas, thoughts or beliefs are transmitted. Our environment determines what we shall achieve in life and become. Often, society, friends, and family do not expect much from you because they think they know you. Familiarity is assuming knowledge about something.

If you want to become a leader in your area, you need to become aware of your environment. Watch and guard it. Never keep company with people who tell you that it cannot be done. Leave those people immediately and follow your heart, dreams, and passion. When you follow your heart, you will end up becoming a leader. Do not be afraid of people's negative comments. People will talk about you whether you permit them or not.

5. Wrong Ideas: "The Leaders Of Tomorrow"

I believe the above saying applies to everyone, whether in America, Europe, China, Asia or Africa. It was a typical statement when I was a young student. They told us during functions that we were the "leaders of tomorrow." Inside the young people is a trapped spirit of leadership. That spirit can be destroyed by the culture, brainwashing, and a dangerous environment. I am the firstborn of my parents who have gone to be with the Lord in heaven.

I recall in 2006, my father was leading everything, but immediately he passed on; during our cultural family and clan meeting before the funeral, everyone was looking at me and asking what was supposed to be done. I was asked about the situation of the children, family land, and property and also about the future of our home and family. I was not leading before Papa's death, but inside me was a trapped leader. I believe in every family or community, whenever a person passes on or leaves, someone takes over as a leader. Leadership is trapped inside every person; it is just waiting to be manifested.

6. Failure to Mentor and Coach Future Leaders

I recall a family that had a business worth millions of dollars. When the children grew up and after their parent's died, they sold everything and became bankrupt. The children wasted the wealth in a very short time. In my view, I would have loved the parents to have left a book or an account of their personal history giving insight, information, and knowledge about how the wealth was acquired. History is more important than money. Parents need to change the way they think about succession. They need to leave their knowledge, experiences, and contacts behind so that children can learn from them and assume their destiny.

7. Lack of Passion

Do you Have Passion for Something? There are millions of people without passion for anything. They just drift in life just as river water flows to sea. I believe the lack of passion and drive is a contributing factor of no leadership. What is passion?If you have a passion for something and it seems like you can never get it out of your mind, that is where your gift lies. I recall a high school student named Chelengat from Mbale, Uganda, who was passionate about athletics, particularly long races and ten kilometre races. Whenever he was on the track, he would always win until after secondary education. He was more passionate about running than studying. Running or athletics was his gift that would make him great. If you enjoy something and are willing to do it 24/7, then that is your passion and gift, which will lead you to your leadership position. If you are not doing what you are passionate about, you are going to end up being frustrated.

In addition, every individual has a desire for something. My passion is helping poor people, equipping and empowering leaders to serve humanity. My passion is teaching, training and sharing ideas on leadership, passion, potential, purpose and vision to people. I love sharing with people the things they need to do to become future leaders. I love to inspire people, helping them plan their lives and effectively change the cause of things. I love to mentor and coach people.

What is Your Passion?

True Story of Sports Training at Nelson Mandela Stadium

One time I met a group of footballers and athletes who were training. I saw a young man and woman compete and run together. I went over and told them that they had the potential to become all they wanted to be. I spoke for over 45 minutes to over 45 athletes about the power to succeed and lead. I told them if they were passionate about what they do, they would shake hands with the Uganda President someday, because their gift will bring them before great men. I told them about two Ugandan athletes who were not known at all, but their gifts took them to the State House to meet and dine with the President of Uganda.

Where do You Invest Your Resources?

I have invested a lot resources, both money and time, to study leadership. I spend hours studying theories and books about leadership and management. My interest is to understand why leaders are different and what principles they apply to be a success. I believe that everybody can have a better life and can develop and improve their situation. A person's background does not matter; what matters is the seed inside them. I discovered every time I speak with people, they end up saying, "You inspire and motivate us."

Professor Kupuliano Odaet, Comparative Education

I also read the stories of how one of the men who studied as a student with my mom would walk for 12 km to school and ended up becoming a professor. I am talking about the late Kupuliano Odaet, Professor of Comparative Education. He was a leader in Education Sector in Uganda, including teaching and training students in the School of Education in Makerere University. He was a leader who influenced Uganda's education. Years later, the Ugandan government built secondary schools in every county and they were called Seed Schools.

The Value and Power of Strong Foundation

During my early years, my parents and grandparents encouraged us to read the word of God. In the Bible we learned stories like the birth of Samuel, David killing Goliath, Saul converting to Paul, Stephen's death as a martyr, Peter denying Jesus, Judas Iscariot betraying Jesus, Samson and Delilah, Abraham having no children, Noah building the ark, and many other stories.

When I grew up, I began to think about how they were able to do the things they did. To me, these were great lessons. These experiences changed the way I viewed my world.

Then came the death of my mother in 1987. This was a shocking event to me. During this time, I asked several questions, and I could not get any answers. But through it all, I concluded that:

1. There are questions in life we cannot answer. We cannot explain where the wind is coming from or where it is going. We cannot explain why the Earthquake occurred in Haiti or why flooding took place in Pakistan.

2. There are things in life that, when they happen, we cannot explain. You cannot explain fully why someone divorced you or why someone died. Doctors attempt to explain, but their explanation is more on the how rather than the why.

3. There are things in life we cannot change. We can advise people, but we cannot change them. They must decide to change themselves.

4. There are things in life over which we have no control. We cannot control Earthquakes, floods, drought or other natural disasters.

5. There are things we cannot stop. For instance, we cannot prevent things such as death, a volcanic eruption, flooding, or an Earthquake.

6. There are things in life that we cannot exceed. We have limitations that make us unable to excel at some things.

7. There are things in life for which we are not responsible. For instance, I am not responsible for the decisions my younger brother makes to watch movies instead of reading books on personal development.

When these things happen, don't blame yourself; instead get on with your life and do something to make a difference in the world. The way to navigate through the torrents and storms of life requires you to have some secrets and principles:

1. There are things only God can do. Let God do His will and purpose.

2. There are things only God knows and will only tell you if He wishes. If God does not tell you, you have to leave it to God. It is not your business, but God's business.

3. There are things only God understands. You cannot understand everything God knows. Your brain is finite and too small to understand everything that happens in life.

4. There are things only God can change. You cannot change or add anything to life. Only God changes things in life.

5. There are things for which we as humans or parents are not responsible. Do not blame yourself for these things. Every person is accountable and responsible for their decisions. They are accountable for their decisions and outcomes.

6. They cannot blame anyone for their personal decisions, choices, and actions. Sometimes you take personal responsibility for things you did not decide.

7. There are things only God can explain. I believe only God can explain why Earthquakes, floods, crises or certain things happen in life.

The key to life is doing all you can do and leave the rest to God. Do your best and leave the rest to the One Who has the ultimate power and authority.

The True Keys to Life, Confidence and Success

I believe with all my heart that the key to success and peace is knowing certain things:
- Know your limitations as a person.
- Know your strengths and weaknesses.
- Know the opportunities and threats to your leadership.
- Know that every problem is seasonal and any storm that affects you is temporary.
- Know that there is no problem that is permanent.
- Know that life itself is a mysterious experience; sometimes plans fail.

- Know that you have purpose and potential in life
- Know how to use the potential to change your life.
- Develop a vision for your life and pursue it with faith and planning.
- Believe in the dark and light moments of life. Life offers dark and light moments.
- Life has both opportunities and crises.

The Duty of All Men and Women who Aspire to Lead and Serve

Every person wants to lead and help others. However, the problem in today's world is everyone wants to obtain power and use it in a wrong way. This is one of the evils that has affected every society, and many conflicts in the world are a result of an abuse of power and authority. Some leaders are obsessed with power and are unwilling to give it up.

There are many examples in Africa where leaders are hungry for power and not willing to let it go. As the next generation comes on the scene, there is the need to change these attitudes and practices that have been adopted and accepted.

The Managers Who Never Discovered Their Leadership

I was having lunch one day at Uganda Management Institute and many students were waiting to get lunch. Others were busy eating and chatting with one another. As the number of students increased, I thought and reflected on why the students were there.

75

One of the thoughts that came to me was that the students were pursuing management training. Management training is about learning how to manage people in organizations, which is not the same thing as leadership. It is learning how to handle resources and funds. As the students continued, I realized that most of those who were getting management training were being trained to believe that they can be managers and not leaders. But in my thoughts, I realized all those who were being trained as managers would become leaders if they discovered their leadership gift, vision and serve it to the world.

Servant Leadership Will Make You Influential

Jesus taught his disciples that if you want to be great you must serve. Leadership is about serving people or followers. Jesus was a great example of a servant leader. He served His disciples during the last supper before His crucifixion. He offered and washed the feet of all the disciples. He did it with humility. A servant leader becomes a leader when he or she serves her gift to the world.

In my country, there is an Olympic Gold medallist named Stephen Kiprotich, from Kapchorwa District, about 77 kilometers from where I was born. This guy is a runner. His gift is running. He is an athlete. He won an Olympic gold medal in a 2012 marathon race in London. When he returned to Uganda, Stephen Kiprotich was hosted to a state dinner by the Ugandan President, Yoweri Museveni.

In Africa, meeting the President of a nation is not an easy wish. The President is protected, and very few people have access to him or her. What enabled this unknown athlete to meet the President was not his background or education but his gift. When he excelled in his gift and served it to the world in London, it brought him before great people. This is where King Solomon's words as presented in Proverbs 18:16 come into play: "A man's gift maketh room for him, and bringeth him before great men."

He also won another gold medal at the 14th IAAF World Championships in Athletics (Moscow 2013). In the history of Uganda, Stephen Kiprotich will never be forgotten. Even if he died today, he will remain in the record books as a Ugandan who won an Olympic gold medal and a gold medal at the World Championship. You need to think of doing one simple act that puts your life in the history books.

When you discover the gift God gave you and refine it through work then serve with it, you will impact and influence your generation. You will then become great. Stephen became great not because of his education or luck but because of his gift that he took the time and work to develop. Servant leadership is about giving your gift to the world and passing it on. Do not be arrogant or refuse to serve with your gift. When you accept to serve others, you will get your greatness.

If you want to become the greatest, then the first thing you need to do is to serve with your gift without seeking payments and getting compensated. Seek for an opportunity to volunteer. I have met young graduates who tell me they cannot volunteer. They want to quickly get well-paying jobs. There are many qualified graduates with academic qualifications who have no jobs.

Jesus Christ as The Example of Great Leadership

Jesus Christ, to me, is the greatest leader of all time. He was born in a manger and came from a poor background. He was baptized and filled with Holy Spirit. He was betrayed by a close friend. He died for my sins and yours. He rose from the dead and will come again. He went through the pain of the cross to pay for my sins and yours. He had a group of local people whom he told to follow him. Those people became global leaders and "upturn the world " He had a message, *"I will make you fishers of men."* Jesus taught the disciples about the Kingdom of God using parables and stories. He asked questions. He performed miracles. He healed the blind, sick, and raised the dead. He cursed a fig tree that bore no fruit. He taught the leaders about their assignment, the Great Commission. Jesus taught me lessons about leadership. If you study His principles, you will learn a lot. When I found out about His life, I received an overdose of revelation on what it takes to be a leader.

Who are your mentors and teachers? Why do you want to be a leader?

Everyone Has Capacity to Lead and Leadership

I am convinced that every human being was born with the ability to lead. The problem is, those who are leaders have not been given opportunity to practice and hone that leadership. I was one of those who thought I could never be a leader. In my country, we have men and women who have been appointed to sensitive positions. For example, the Head of State or the President appoints the commander of the army. The person who is appointed commander of the army did not get the position because of looks but because he has undergone military training. Anyone who does not have military training or experience in the military is not appointed to this position.

I believe the appointing authority knows that if a person has no knowledge or experience in that field, they cannot be effective. The head of security, for example, is named a leader because of the experience, skills, and knowledge he has in security related matters. The same goes for pastors, priests or managing directors. Every person can lead, but most people never find their leadership spot because of several factors such as fear, bad company, bad friends, associations, groups, beliefs, training, education and fear of failure or bad character.

Before, I move to the next chapter, I would like to share the following story.

The Story Of Young Lions, The Cubs

I recall one day I was watching the National Geographic Channel, which showed a lioness giving birth and the whole life of that lioness with her cubs. As the cubs grew, the lioness would play with them. The lioness would go hunting; then after the kill, she would bring the meat for the young ones to eat. As time passed by, the cubs were taken out to learn how to catch and hunt for prey. After the training, the young ones became kings of the jungle. The young lions became what they were created to be.

When you observe the young lions, you can see the "king of the jungle" in them long before they are ready to assume that position. The same is true of you as well. You may not be what you want to become yet. You do not believe that there is a leader in you, but everyone has that leadership spirit that just needs to be cultivated. The leadership spirit is the natural gift to lead.

The Pastor's Daughter Becomes a Leader

In 1999, I was hired as a Project Director in one of the Projects in a remote village in Busiula, under the Church of God in Bugiri in Eastern Uganda. Bugiri is about 70 kilometres from the source of the Nile in Jinja.

I traveled to the duty station in Bugiri and took over the post of Project Director. I recall during my interaction with family and the children, I said something like this, "One of these kids will be the next leader and even be a Member of Parliament (MP)." I saw in these kids the ability and potential to become anything God created them to be. A decade after the conversation, one of the girls in the project became a Female Member of the Parliament representing Namayingo District in 9th Parliament of Uganda. The reason why you need to respect people in your environment is that you do not know what is inside of them. Trapped inside every person is a leader.

Whenever I come across people and start a discussion about leadership, I notice that most believe that only a few are born leaders, and think they cannot lead. I have come to appreciate this experience because I was like them, but not only can you lead, you must lead and you should lead.

A leader emerges or is born when they achieve self-discovery and an understanding of self. A leader is born when a person's past no longer determines or affects their future. A leader is born when they discover their gift, grow and serve it to the world.

Everyone is Created With Leadership Potential on The Inside

- Every human being is created by God to lead. This is why people do not want to be oppressed. It is because there is a domination spirit inside every human. People were told to dominate when God created Adam.

- Every person can be trained, mentored and coached to become a leader and to lead. There has been misconceptions about leadership that some are born leaders and others are created to be followers. The truth is every one willing to learn can be trained to lead. I will give you an example of a lay reader who starts reading the Bible in church, then goes to the seminary, becomes a priest or reverend, and ends up becoming the head of a church.

- Even though humans were created with a leadership potential and spirit, most of them will die with their leadership potential. A couple of individuals are afraid of becoming leaders. People are also afraid of their culture or negative comments from other people. People are afraid of their background or their past. The past is a weight that has kept people from stepping into their destiny and their vision.

- Every leader has a destination and a legacy to leave behind. What does your past look like? Is it a good one? Do you think it is a horrible one or will people regret when you are gone? It is time to change it and repent; apologize before you are gone. When you die, people will bury you; but as they walk away from your grave; they will bear your character in mind.

- The world needs the leadership that is trapped inside you. The world is full of needs that must be met, problems that require solutions but the person to serve that gift is the leader in you. Every human has leadership trapped inside.

- In every follower, there is a leader that has been trapped inside and not yet manifested and revealed. If you believe and accept what people will tell you, you will become trapped and fail to show up your leadership. You are like a seed. Every seed has a tree inside of it, just as every egg has a chicken inside it.

4

Know Why You Need To Lead

If you do not change direction,
you may end up where you are heading.
Lao Tzu

The Necessity for Leaders and Leadership

The world is in turmoil right now. There is no safe haven except the kingdom of heaven where God dwells. In the USA, several unarmed citizen have been killed by police. In Iraq, Syria, South Sudan, Somalia, and Nigeria, people are dying like flies. Tens of thousands of individuals have been displaced and uprooted from their homes. There is fear and terror everywhere. When you travel through international airports, security personnel check to ensure you do not have a knife or some other weapon.

I was traveling from Nairobi to Entebbe through Jomo Kenyatta International Airport (JKIA) in 2016. One of my mentors from World Food Program had given me a gift way back in 2006. The gift was a key holder with a cutter that had a logo of the World Food Program. It was a beautiful gift. When I arrived at the JKIA,

I forgot to check it in my luggage and had carried it in a small bag. As the security officer was checking my luggage, they found the key holder. They told me there were two options: either I go back to the check-in counter and check it in as luggage or I give it to them and lose it. Looking at the time I had left to board the airplane, it was too late. I had no choice but to surrender the key chain. I had been carrying and keeping this precious key holder for years, and I lost it just like that.

I thought to myself. What is the problem with the world? I have never thought of killing any human in my life, and that key chain was so small that it could be used to harm anybody. But the world, has people with such motives. Are you that kind of person? If you have selfish motives of destruction or killing people, you are not fit to be a leader.

I recall when my grandparents lost their son and daughter, and someone was suspected of killing them. They told us as kids that God will revenge the wrong. I did not know how that would happen. I thought to myself God would come with a knife and kill that person. But later I learned that God's ways are not our ways and His thoughts are not our thoughts. I concluded at that time that the need for leaders today is far greater than it used to be. Leaders are needed to address issues such: poverty, terrorism and many more. There is a global outcry for leaders and leadership.

Among many reasons why leaders are needed are:

1. Provide Direction

When you watch the news headlines, you will notice many issues that require leadership. You will hear people who are

84

seeking for a mandate to lead and make the lives of their people better. You will hear one candidate attacking the other. Those in opposition are attacking those in government and vice versa. But those leaders who seek a mandate have disappointed the voters.

Those leaders abuse the power entrusted to them and are utterly corrupt. They are ideologically bankrupt and have no capacity to come up with solutions to improve the lives of their people. They are unable to solve the problems people face.

In Uganda, every five years several people are nominated from either the party level or the electoral commission to become a candidate. The electoral commission will then announce the election roadmap. There will be people who traverse the country, wooing people for votes, and when the campaign period is over, they will forget those who elected them. As a result, the problems persist and remain.

2. Guide in Decisions and Actions

Leaders are needed in government, business, military, schools, universities, and churches. The type of leaders needed are those who are effective and do the right thing. There is a difference between a good thing and right things. Every person needs to rise to the occasion and become one of those leaders who does the right thing. You must become one of those active leaders who has the best interests of the people you are leading. Leaders are needed in financial, education, health, social, environmental, politics and defence sectors, among others.

3. Provide Hope During Dark Moments

During dark moments or crises, people lose hope and despair. Fear makes people engage in acts that are against civility. A mother of three children will sell her body to get money for food. A young girl will sell her body to men. A young man will break into a shop or rob a bank. In dark moments, effective leaders must lead people and provide hope.

If you study history, you will notice the story of Sir Winston Churchill who was the British Prime Minister during World War II. He provided motivating leadership to the people of Great Britain during a time of great tribulation. His speech following the near disaster at Dunkirk was one for the ages. Nelson Mandela is another leader that stood the test and defeated apartheid in South Africa. He led the black South African majority and white minority to a place of reconciliation and apartheid was abolished. In Scripture, we have David as a leader who fought to defeat Goliath and established a city called Jerusalem. There are other leaders like Joshua, Moses, Daniel, Ruth, and Nehemiah who led their people during the darker moments of life.

4. Provide Vision, Wisdom, and Purpose

A leader is always in front. A leader needs to have vision and personal purpose. It is imperative that a leader be competent and skilled. A leader must be a person who lives by a set of standards and principles. A leader must have the conviction to a cause and not compromise in order to succeed. A leader must have the wisdom to guide the followers through the challenges of the world today. A leader must be an intellectual and a reader. He must be willing to learn and should be teachable. We need leaders who believe in God, not the things of the world that pass away. We need leaders who do not think of themselves. Wisdom does not come from man but from God.

In James 1:5, God promised that if anyone lacks wisdom, let him ask from God who gives it generously. King Solomon received wisdom when he asked God for wisdom to lead the nation of Israel. If you are a leader, where is the source of your knowledge? Does it come from God or your wealth? 1 Kings 4:29 says, *"And God gave Solomon wisdom and understanding exceeding much, and largeness of heart, even as the sand that is on the seashore."* Our leaders need to ask God for wisdom to lead effectively and make wise decisions.

I believe that every human need could be fulfilled if everyone were to seek wisdom, work to unleash their potential and consistently seek God's guidance. Every person was conceived for a reason, and that reason is to make a difference in the world.

Everything will improve if there is true leadership. Everything will fail if the leaders are absent and ineffective. Nations improve or progress because of leadership. School or families advance if there is leadership. Communities improve, develop and progress when there is leadership. If you see problems in your community, it means there is a leadership vacuum.

What other reasons, do you think leaders are needed in your community, organization or nation?

5

How To Become The Greatest

To win, you have to believe you will win.
Lailah Gift Akita

Who is the Greatest?

Have you ever thought about greatness? The disciples of Jesus asked that question on greatness over two thousand years ago. They were with their leader, Jesus and they started to argue and debate about who was the greatest. In other words, they want to know who the second in command to Jesus Christ was. Jesus answered this question by using a figurative story. He said if anyone wanted to be great, he must become like a little child (Mark 9:35).

Some Leaders Own Followers, as They Lead

Some of the people who claim to be leaders own their followers; they treat their followers like benefactors. They believe the bigger the number of followers, the greater their leadership influence, and that defines their greatness.

These are dangerous beliefs, attitudes, and practices. Jesus spoke about the issue of owning followers. In Luke 22:24-27, there is a conversation between the disciples that borders on who the greatest was among them.

Now there was also a dispute among them, as to which of them should be considered the greatest. And He said to them, *"The kings of the Gentiles exercise lordship over them, and those who exercise authority over them are called 'benefactors.' But not so among you; on the contrary, he who is greatest among you let him be as the younger, and he who governs as he who serves. For who is greater, he who sits at the table, or he who serves? Is it not he who sits at the table? I am among you as the One who serves."* (Luke 22: 24-27)

Jesus heard their arguments, and He had to correct their wrong philosophy and ideology. He told them the Gentile's exercise lordship, which means ownership. Jesus did not rebuke the desire of greatness, but did rebuke the process for which a person becomes great. It was about lordship. Lordship means owning.

There is another story that reveals what happens when we fix our hearts that service being greatness(The full account is found in Matthew 20:20-28). The two brothers were doing the same thing we see happening all over the world today. They wanted to get into leadership positions without serving their friends. The result of desiring greatness for greatness' sake means people will sell their bodies for sex to their bosses. People will violate their consciousness to get greatness. People will bribe voters to get to Parliament or the national assembly. People abuse the trust of their followers to get power and be called great. This belief in how to achieve greatness needs to change.

God the Creator, created every person to be great and dominate the world in some area. He created people to work, and through service, they become great. If you study Jesus' concept of greatness, He taught the disciples that it comes through service.

Being Ambitious: Is it Good or Bad?

Being ambitious is not a bad thing provided the ambition does not destroy the potential of the people around you. Being ambitious reveals the need to advance and become great, but it has to pass through a process where integrity and Godly principles are obeyed and applied. Ambition is an inherent desire that is healthy and provides opportunities for human development.

Using the analogy of a seed or tree, it always wants to grow and become bigger. The desire to become great is the source of one's reason for existence or purpose. Therefore, to be great is good; it must be achieved with integrity and not through covert ways, corruption or abuse of power. It must be achieved through merit and approval by God.

Todays "Leaders" Never Tell all The Truth to Followers

I was working on this book when a group of religious leaders came to the dining hall for lunch at Olive Garden in Bugolobi in Kampala. They were part of a group called the Uganda Governance Monitoring Platform. As I sat at the corner of the dining hall, I watched and listened to what was going on. These leaders were representatives of many of the different religious groups in Uganda. Some of the leaders were elderly, while others were younger but middle-aged men. There were women in the group. The religious leaders included Christians and Muslims. One of the leaders spoke openly about his grievances and concerns about leadership in Uganda. They talked about a leader's decision to change the term limits stipulated in the constitution of Uganda in 1996. The 1996 Constitution of Uganda provided two five-years terms for the presidency.

One of the leaders said that by 2004, there were rumors, about the change in term limits, and when President Museveni was asked about it, he denied the rumor and warned those who were spreading it. But what followed in 2005 was entirely different from the message the president gave. In 2005, the term limits that allowed the leader to contest or run for the presidency as he wishes to lead the country were removed from the constitution. I thought about the kind of leaders we have. Can our leaders be trusted to keep their words? Do you keep changing your viewpoints? A true leader keeps his or her words. One of the leaders, a bishop, said to his reverends that he should not to tell the whole truth. What a comment!

What kind of leaders do you have in your country, church or organization?

Examples of True Leaders That You Must Know

When you study the great leaders of influence during the last century, you will notice there were those who were servants and others who oppressed their followers. I want to list some of the leaders whom I call servant leaders that have made a difference: Mother Teresa, Nelson Mandela, Kwame Nkrumah, Abraham Lincoln, Dr.Martin Luther King Jr., Thomas Edison, Helen Keller, Mahatma Gandhi, Steven Jobs, and Bill Gates. This is by no means a comprehensive list, but all these names are examples of great leaders who impacted the world.

Are you going to make the list of influential leaders? Are you an individual who makes a difference in your community? Are you making a difference? When you carefully study the people listed above, you will notice that they were true leaders in their own right. Some of them did not even have degrees; all they had was their purpose, and they pursued it. They became leaders through discovering, developing, refining and serving the people they led.

There is something surprising about these people. None of them ever aspired to be great, but instead they concentrated on pursuing their purpose. They were occupied with pursuing and developing their gifts and went on to serve the world. For example, Bill Gates dropped out of school and the teacher said he was suffering from Attention Deficit Hyperactivity Disorder (ADHD), but he was just an intelligent young boy who was ahead of the teachers and knew things they did not know or understand. He had a gift which he pursued, and today Bill Gates is the richest man in the world.

Gates discovered his gift and served it to the world. His gift was Microsoft and his Windows operating system, which caused software desgners to adopt a universal standard for commands. For example, today CTRL-S means save, but before Windows, every programmer used their own shortcut, making it a nightmare for users who had to use different commands for each program.

How Can You Become Great?

When I was a young child, I wanted to run all the countries in the world. When I went to school, I wanted to be a class monitor, and I always wanted to speak to other people. As I grew older, I saw there was a problem. Some people told me I could not ever be great. I was told that I was too proud and did not deserve to be great.

As I went to high school and college, I learned that becoming great was through winning an election or fighting. I had people who were struggling to win an election and I participated in elections at college. I was elected to a tribal association called TESO Students Development Association (TESDA) as an education secretary in Makerere University. TESDA was the largest union of students hailing from Teso sub-region in Uganda. At the end of my university education, I handed over the post to those leaders who were ready to take over.

Service is the Key to Greatness

The secret to greatness does not come through manipulation, control or the use of power. It comes through service of your gift to those around you. In Mathew 20:26-27, Jesus says, *"Not so with you. Instead, whoever wants to become great among you must be your servant and whoever wants to be the first must be your slave."* This statement does not advocate for slavery as we know it, but rather refers to a person who voluntarily becomes a slave of the gift. The person who is a servant will be the greatest because the greatest has a gift that he or she serves. When a gift is served, it makes the person serving great.

When you read the great philosophers like Plato, Socrates or even management gurus like Peter Drucker on greatness, their ideas are radically different from those that Jesus Christ advanced and taught his followers. Jesus Christ's ideas on greatness are written in Luke 22:26, Matthew 23:11 and Mark 10:43. Jesus Christ's idea about greatness is the best model, for it does not make another human superior over others. I have never seen a servant who is manipulative, controlling, or power hungry.

However, I have observed that most leaders in our world continue to adopt and apply the Greek ideas about leadership. They are good at manipulating, controlling and oppressing those they lead. The idea of greatness and leadership that Jesus Christ presented has not the slightest thing to do with ruling, manipulating, oppressing or controlling followers. Its central idea is that a leader serves the gift to the world and greatness is a side-benefit. As you serve, your followers, they will give their trust to you to lead them. You get the authority to lead the followers through service. That is true leadership.

Changing the Mindset

When I began to study the radical views that Jesus Christ taught His disciples, I thought to myself that the ideas he espoused requires a paradigm shift. The worldview of leadership or greatness is based on the number of people controlled or the number of individuals under the leader. It depends on the number of individuals that obey, follow or respect you. How many people give you reports or are in your political party? How many people do you intimidate and influence? These ideas of leadership are satanic and devilish. Looking at it objectively, Hitler was a great leader, but his ideas were satanic because he used those who followed him to accomplish his evil ends to kill people. Then, when his followers, the German people, were no longer of any use to them, he discarded them, calling for a "Scorched Earth policy" and genocide against his own people, feeling they had proven themselves unworthy of surviving.

The Process of Measuring Leadership in our World

The numbers in a political rally and other favourable statistics does not necessarily mean that you are great leader. It might just be saying that you are a good and expert dictator, manipulator or oppressor. I was in one nation during election season and I asked local people about the massive crowds a particular leader was generating. The followers said that they were paid and transported to the rally. Leadership and greatness does not come from the number of people that follow the leader; instead it originates from those served and those who are faithful. One day Jesus said in Mathew 20:28, *"Just as the Son of Man did not come to be served, but to serve, and give his life as a ransom for many."* Leaders are the servants of the people, not themselves.

The Youngest Becomes the Greatest

Luke 22:26 says, *"But you are not to be like that. Instead, the greatest among you should be like the youngest and the one who rules like the one who serves."* The world taught that a leader is to compel people to follow him. Now, Jesus Christ comes along and shifts or changes this universal message. It is generally easy to get people to do what you want them to do. They can be sent to do something and they will gladly do it because children have a natual desire to please those in authority. But if you tell adults to do something, they will demand money, payment or some kind of a reward.

The Power of a Leadership Gift

What is a gift? It is your skills, talents, abilities and capacities, something that no other person can take from you because it is an intricate part of who you are. The most important thing a person needs is to discover his or her gift and start developing it. If while young you developed your gifts, it means people will think of you when they need that gift. When you need a doctor, you do not think about your plumber. If you do not develop your gift, nobody will look for you. If people know that you are able to get things done and produce the results they need, they will look for you because they know that is your gift.

In my own experience, every time there was a problem in our family or with relatives, they always sought my advice. I recall one time, when my counsin Caroline Atim was diagnosed with a kidney problem that required a transplant. My family came to my house and said I needed to do something for Caroline because her life was at risk. I chaired a meeting and agreed on the way forward. I made arrangements to send a donor to Aghakan Hospital in Kenya for some additional tests that were needed before traveling to India for the kidney transplant. Today, as I write this book, my sister, the mother of two young handsome boys, is doing well and has fully recovered.

Another related story happened when my cousin, Lugard was diagnosed with TB in Mbale Hospital in Eastern Uganda. He was put on a treatment regimen that lasted eight months. Afterwards, it was assumed that he had recovered.

However, two months after completing an eight-month treatment, Lugard started complaining again and had a constant cough. His mother called me and said, "There is nobody who can take care of Lugard except you. If you do not help Lugard, we shall lose him." I told them to send him to Kampala so that I could take him to Mulago National Hospital for treatment and attention. He recovered. Were it not for my willingness to be a servant to my cousin, he would have passed on.

Some people might say I am special, fortunate or lucky. I do not feel special. I have several cousins and brothers who have the same abilities as me, but they are always coming to me. Why is that? I believe I have a gift to help, serve and assist people. I have helped strangers and worked with large humanitarian organizations supporting thousands of vulnerable people. If you want to be great, the way you get to rule or dominate is through being willing to serve people all the time.

Proverbs 18:16 says, *"A gift opens the way for the giver and ushers him into the presence of the great."* Whenever I read this verse as a teenager, I kept wondering what is my gift. When I was a young Christian, I read the story of Joseph in Genesis 41. The leader of Egypt called Joseph and said he was told Joseph could interpret dreams. The leader wanted the gift that Joseph had. It does not matter where you come from, or what your background is; if you have a gift and people hear of it, they will look up to you for the gift. The gift makes you valuable. Nobody can make you great, but if you have a gift, it will make you great if you humble yourself and are willing to use it properly.

I recall growing up in rural Uganda; as a young boy, I never thought I would fly in an airplane. But God had given me the gift of reading, studying and the ability to work. Through reading, studying and working hard, I was able to get the knowledge, skills, and competencies that enabled me to work with the United Nations. Everybody admires those who work with the United Nations in my country, but it is not easy to get your foot in the door.

Today, through that knowledge, I have been able to visit countries I never expected and meet people in a way I have never dreamed possible. Every human being has a gift that he or she comes to the Earth with. The problem is many people never discover that gift and it ends up being unused in their lives. A gift will give you opportunities to overcome obstacles.

How can you Develop your Leadership Gift?

There are many ways to develop your gift.

1. Observation and Close Monitoring

Through observing others, you can begin to develop the gift that you have. You need to observe those who might have the same gift as you and learn from them. You should not try to become like them but be yourself. For example, if you have a gift in football, you need to observe and learn from great footballers. You can also seek opportunities to interview them and learn from them.

2. Reading

Another way to develop your gift is by reading about your ideal gift. There are many great books or even websites that can help you get the information you need. You will get the knowledge, skills and the competencies required to improve your gift. I know most people do not like reading books, but if you desire to achieve anything of lasting value, you have to invest time in reading. The Apostle Paul told young Timothy to *"give attendance to reading"* (1 Timothy 4:13). The choice is yours.

3. Talk About it

You can also talk to some people about your desire, or you can speak to a person who is doing something which you are interested. However, you need to be careful whom you talk, particularly your family or friends, because some of them will try to discourage you. However, there are many people who like to speak about their achievements and how they got there. You need to ask about the knowledge they got, the skills required and abilities necessary for the gift to grow. You can also keep on practicing your gift.

4. Ask and Get Feedback

You can also seek feedback from those willing to give you honest feedback. When you get honest feedback, you will become aware of your knowledge, skills or abilities, and most importantly; your strengths and weaknesses. There is a 360 degree tool that is used to assess senior managers; you can get it online and send it to trusted people to get feedback. You need to ask many people to give you feedback and do not be afraid or resentful of what they tell you. After you get feedback, develop an action plan to improve the weaker areas. An action plan is simply your next plan of action for improvement.

5. Self-Reflection and Meditation

Through this approach, you can improve your gift. You need to reflect on things you can do. You need to devote time to know the hidden things about you. You must find moments for thinking or reflecting on the issues you need to better yourself. Reflection allows you to have an opportunity to recall things that are important in your life.

6. Seek to Add Value

When you invest your time and resources while seeking value, you will end up developing your gift. When you are valuable, your net worth will go up. Seeking value is like seeking knowledge. Finding value is like training hard to win a competition. Most people do not want to pay the price and expect to have an improvement in their lives, thinking it will just happen. When you seek value and become valuable, you will automatically become significant and important to your generation.

Suppose the organization you are working with or for avoids calling or giving you work. This means there is a problem with you in that organization. It means either you are not a person who gets the work done or you have no gift. The word "doing" means executing and "done" is the same as execute. The term "executive"; comes from executing. An executive is a person who can get things done.

When an organization or a company is having problems or a crisis and begins to lose money, often the first person fired is the top executive. Why? The executive was unable to get things done. In the USA, during election season, the country will look to a president who will fix the problems the country is going through.

Why People Never Develop Their Leadership Gifts?

There are many reasons why millions of people never develop their gifts, achieve their desires and live effectively. Here are some of the reasons:

1. Laziness

Most people are lazy. If you are lazy and hate work, you cannot develop your gift. The Bible reveals that there is only one type of person that God does not use, a lazy person. God has used liars, murderers, adulterers, people who have denied Him and hated Him, but there is no record in the Bible of God ever using a lazy person. The Book of Proverbs shows that God hates people who are lazy. Laziness brings poverty. As a young man, I found in Scripture where it says lazy hands bring in poverty. Some people are poor because they do not want to work. Through work, you can develop your ability and gifts will be manifested.

2. Irresponsibility

Another thing people run away from is responsibility. Responsibility gives you the ability to respond. The majority of individuals want the privleges that come with leadership but none of the responsibilities. They do not understand their roles and what they are supposed to do.

3. Avoiding responsibilities

There are also people who avoid or hide from responsibility. When you are willing to be responsible, God will make you great. Great people are 'response-ability' people. I mean they are responsible. They are trustworthy and dependable. If a person avoids responsibility, that person is making room to fail in the development of their potential.

4. Inconsistency

Human beings are interesting people or creatures. They dream of doing big things, but many never want to put in the required work to achieve their dreams. We have several examples of individuals who are inconsistent and easily distracted from what needs to be accomplished. Because of this habit, they never do anything and fail to discover their true potential and gift.

Servant Leadership Must be Taught to the Present and Next Generation

There are many theories on leadership that professors have taught to their students. I recommend that the servant leadership model be taught in all schools or business management schools, so that current and future leader's mindsets are tilted to be servants. Many colleges produce leaders who are not interested in service but want to serve their own interests. If an individual or corporate organisation wants to become great, it must strive to become a servant within its community. The corporations should not be exclusively focused on profits or revenues; they need to also ask how they can serve their clients or customers better.

An organization that strives to practice servant leadership will eventually become a great company. Many organizations have collapsed because they forgot to serve their clients. Even individuals who fail in leadership positions, fail because they do not serve their clients and only serve themselves. Defective corporations exploit people.

The Fundamental Principles for Servant Leadership

I am always motivated by understanding and seeking to gain knowledge. Years back, I learned that wisdom is better than knowledge. You can have knowledge but still be foolish. For example, knowledge is knowing that cigarettes cause cancer while wisdom is deciding to quit. Experience should make you a wise person. I believe the more you study and read, the more knowledge you gain, which can be helpful, but the application of that knowledge gives you wisdom.

1. Servant leaders know that God Created All Humans to be Leaders

God does not prefer some people to be leaders and others followers. To be a leader does not mean you do something. It is something you manifest. Leaders do not retire, they transfer leadership to the next generation.

2. Servant leaders know that God prepares people for leadership.

God prepared a place for you before He created you. You should not go looking for the leadership position like the sons of Zebedee did.

3. Servant leaders know that there is a price to pay for leadership

Getting to your leadership position will require paying a price. Jesus said, "You will indeed drink from my cup... can you drink the cup I am going to drink?" "We can", they answered. There is no leadership without somebody paying the price. It has been said, "I you succeed without suffering, it is only because somebody else suffered without succeeding." To become a leader, you will have to prepare, train, develop, and refine your skills. The leadership position is prepared for you by God, but for you to take it, you have to prepare yourself for it.

4. Servant leaders know that every person has leadership capacity

Leadership is inherent in every person. You cannot pray to God for leadership or request it because you were wired and born as a leader. It all depends on you, whether or not you decide to prepare, develop or utilize it. We can decide what we want to become. We can decide to follow our culture or tradition. But if you choose to follow God, your leadership will be manifested.

5. Servant leaders know that God gives authority for leadership

God has divine power. We cannot give anyone a gift but each person is unique. It is deposited by God using divine power. God arranges that, and nobody can give you a gift or change the position chosen by God.

6. Servant leaders know that leadership is service

You do not lead for yourself. To lead means that you serve others; therefore, leading is service.

7. Servant leaders know themselves

Leadership does not mean doing something but becoming something for others to enjoy. If you want to become yourself, it means you have to discover yourself and this is a process. It takes time.

The Self-Discovery Process

- Who am I?
- What is my gift?
- In what area can I serve?
- How can I serve with my gift?
- Who can I serve with my gift?
- When can I serve with my gift?
- Where have you been?
- What brought you to this point?
- Where are you going?

6

The Value And Power Of Leadership Influence

*The people you have around you
are your greatest influence.*
R.J. Mitte

What is Influence?

Influence is having the ability to affect other people's characters, values, habits, traits, and behaviors. Influence is also the ability of an individual or group of people to impact others and change their lives positively or negatively. Influence is the ability to dominate and impact your generation, such that the death of a leader does not erase the works of that leader. In otherwords, a leader legacy lives on after they are gone.

Also, influence is the capacity to affect the people around the leader and manage circumstances and events. Influence occurs because the leader has the capacity and ability to perform the leadership functions. Influence produces impact and inspiration. An influential person is the one who followers respect, believe and and seek counsel.

Every human being is being influenced by one person or another. A person who has influence has dominion over those who listen or follow him or her. Influential people inspire followers to follow them from known to unknown.

Jesus Christ is one of the greatest examples of a leader Who influenced the world. Today, people everywhere continue thinking and speaking about His name. His name is still spoken in many languages for over 2,000 years since His ascension to Heaven.

Be Fruitful, Multiply and Dominate

In my search for wisdom and knowledge, I made the Bible the most important book in my life. The three words above are what I believe is the origin of human influence. Being fruitful means to bring forth fruits just like a mango tree bears mangoes. Multiply means to reproduce what you have already, just like Bill Gates dominated the software industry. Your influence will only be possible when you become fruitful in an area of your gift; then you can reproduce that influence until you dominate. You will have dominion when you have become fruitful and multiply your gifts to benefit the human race.

Our True Vine is God

There is a story which Jesus Christ told His disciples in John 15 that illustrates the power of influence:

> I am the true vine, and My Father is the vinedresser. Every branch in me that does not bear fruit He takes away; and every branch that bears fruit He prunes, that it may bear more fruit. You are already clean because of the word which I have spoken to you. Abide in Me, a the branch

cannot bear the fruit in itself, unless it abides in the vine, neither can you, unless you abide in me. "I am the vine, you are the branches. He who abides in me, and I in him bears much fruit; for without me you can do nothing. If anyone does not abide in me, he is cast out as a branch and is withered; and they gather them and throw them into the fire, and they are burned. If you abide in me, and my words abide in you, you will ask what you desire, and it shall be done for you. By this My Father is glorified, that you bear much fruit; so you will be my disciples. (John 15:1-8)

What lessons and insights have you learned from this passage?

I believe to become an influence you must remain attached to the vine. We are told we are the branches. When you look at trees, do you see the branches? Can the branch exist without a stem or roots? Influence comes from being attached to God. A tree cannot produce fruits unless it is connected to the soil. If you abide in God's word, you will ask anything, and it shall be given unto you.

Love and Joy Perfected

As the Father loved Me, I also have loved you; abide in my love. If you keep my commandments, you will abide in my love, just as I have kept My Father's commandments and abide in His love. These things I have spoken to you, that my joy may remain in you, and that your joy may be full. This is my commandment that you love one another as I have loved you. Greater love has no one than this than to lay down one's life for his friends. You are My friends if you do whatever I command you. No longer do I call you servants, for a servant, does not know what his master is doing; but I have called you friends, for all things that I heard from My Father I have made known to you. You did not choose me, but I chose you and appointed you that you should go and bear fruit and that your fruit should remain, that whatever you ask the Father in My name He may give you. These things I command you, that you love one another. (John 15:9-17)

Obedience to God will make you influential, while disobedience will destroy your legacy, influence, authority and leadership. Think about Samson and other leaders whose influence was cancelled. Disobedience will destroy not only you, but also those who follow you. Leadership involves friendship with followers. Jesus, the Leader of the twelve disciples, called them His friends and influenced them to believe in His message.

True Leaders Will be Hated and Persecuted

Jesus said things that were controversial or unpleasant to hear. He said the world hated Him and therefore we should expect to be hated, for we are not different. When you become an influence, you will be hated. When people believe in you, the world will hate you. When people are persuaded by your beliefs, you will be attacked by the world. The secret is getting ready for persecution. Jesus' message of world hatred is in John 15:18-25.

He also said a servant would not be greater than the master, meaning we should not expect to be treated better than He was. But is it possible for a servant to become a master through service? Joseph was a servant and a prisoner in Egypt and ended up in the second highest job in the land. You can be a servant now in your office, community or organization. Continue with the right attitude; your elevation and promotion are on the way.

True Leaders Will Always be Rejected

But when the Helper comes, whom I shall send to you from the Father, the Spirit of truth who proceeds from the Father, He will testify of Me. And you also will bear witness, because you have been with Me from the beginning. (John 15:26-27)

What is "Rejection?"

In this scripture, coming rejection means you will be rejected. Your friends or close associates will disassociate from you. Some of the folks you trust right now will do diabolical things that will break up the relationship. They will do things that will "rock the boat" and destroy the friendship because your strong convictions and integrity will be seen as a threat to them. Are you ready or prepared for rejection? To become an influence, sometimes will come with rejection. Jesus was rejected by His friends, but He focused on His vision and that made Him impatful.

Are you willing to face rejection?

Why is Influence Significant?

People who affected history had influence in their generation, and they were aware of what they wanted in life. They are goal-oriented and had the ability to make priorities and choose from several alternatives. Influential people are impactful but not popular or famous. A good example of this is a man by the name of Ed Kimball. Mr. Kimball was a Sunday School teacher at Mount Vernon Congregational Church. One day, a young boy attended the Sunday School class. The young boy was Bible illiterate and couldn't find the epistle of John in the Bible. That young boy's name was D. L. Moody.

Here is the account of Kimball's using his leadership gift to change the world.

"I started down town to Holton's shoe store," says Mr. Kimball. "When I was nearly there, I began to wonder whether I ought to go just then, during business hours. And I thought maybe my mission might embarrass the boy, that when I went away the other clerks might ask who I was, and when they know who I was they might taunt Moody and ask if I was trying to make a good boy out. of him. While I was pondering over it all, I passed the store without noticing it. Then when I found I had gone by the door, I determined to make a dash for it and have it over at once. I found Moody in the back part of the store wrapping up shoes in paper and putting them on shelves. I went up to him and put my hand on his shoulder, and as I leaned over I placed my foot upon a shoe box. Then I made my plea, and I feel that it was really a very weak one. I don't know just what words I used, nor could Mr. Moody tell. I simply told him of Christ's love for him and the love Christ wanted in return. That was all there was of it. I think Mr. Moody said afterward that there were tears in my eyes. It seemed that the young man was just ready for the light that then broke upon him, for there at once in the back of that shoe store in Boston the future great evangelist gave himself and his life to Christ."

Today, almost no one knows the name Ed Kimbell, but the world knows D.L. Moody, the great evangelist who shook England and America for God, bringing over a million souls to Jesus Christ through his famous revivals. Moody's influence is still being felt today, but it never would have happened were it not for Ed Kimball finding the courage to use his gift.

Jesus Christ as an Impactful and Influential Leader

Jesus Christ was not popular with the Roman and the religious leaders during His time on Earth. He was accused of violating the laws of the land. In John 9, Jesus Christ healed a blind man, but rather than been excited about that, the religious leaders attacked and excommunicated the blind man. The Pharisees called Jesus Christ a sinner, but the blind man was not bothered by this.

Instead, the blind man said, *"It does not matter, all I know is I was blind, but now I can see."*

Jesus Christ impacted the life of the blind man and changed his life. Those who were against Jesus Christ were the elites, called the Pharisees. It is usually the elites in your neighborhood or those who are educated who attack a person of influence that leads in a way contrary to the way they think things should be done. Jesus Christ's work and the account of His life is written in the Gospel. He will not be forgotten and will live forever. Jesus Christ was influential and impactful.

Can you think about your life for a moment? Do you have anybody you have influenced and impacted in your generation? If you are going to create impact and influence your generation, you will need to develop and know your purpose in life. You will need to write it down and pursue it. When you pursue your purpose, you will make a big difference, and you will not be forgotten.

The Danger of Social Media

There are millions of people who are spending hours on Facebook, Twitter, LinkedIn and other social networks. These people waste and abuse time that could better be used to impact and influence their generation. Recent research in the USA revealed that the average young person spends about nine hours a day on social media. Social media has been reported to promote cyber bullying and cybercrime. It has also been linked to obesity since children no longer play and interact face to face with their friends.

Social media has also promoted pornography and illicit relationships. What kind of relationships do you have? What is the impact of those relationships to your goals? Review the quality of your relationships and check if they are beneficial to you.

The Parable of the Sower

On the same day, Jesus went out of the house and sat by the sea. And great multitudes were gathered together to Him so that He got into a boat and sat, and the whole multitude stood on the shore. Then He spoke many things to them in parables, saying: "Behold, a sower went out to sow. and as he sowed, some seed fell by the wayside, and the birds came and devoured them. Some fell on stony places, where they did not have much Earth; and they immediately sprang up because they had no depth of Earth. But when the sun was up they were scorched, and because they had no root, they withered away. And some fell among thorns, and the thorns sprang up and choked them. But others fell on good ground and yielded a crop: some a hundredfold, some sixty, some thirty. He who has ears to hear let him hear!" - (Matthew 13:1-9)

Fundamental Principles from the Parable of the Sower

The Parable of the Sower impacted my life as a young teenager. The sower is doing something that I did as a child and even in adulthood. Seeds have a tendency to grow wherever they are thrown or sown. When you plant or sow seeds on good soil, they will germinate and yield crops that carry future life. If you are going to impact the world, you need to be a sower.

If you were to be a seed, what kind of seed do you want to become? In my experience, a good seed is one that yields fruit and multiplies. Look at your life today and see if you have any fruit. If not, then you need to change your life and start to grow and yield good crops.

Become an excellent sower and constantly sow excellent seeds. That means you need to think of a business idea and become an expert in that business. You have birds that will eat some of the seeds, but enough will survive to perpetuate the next generation. Seeds will fall on rocky soil, on the road and others on good soil. Keep sowing your seeds. Your seeds could be your gift. Do not allow small disappointments or little things make you to miss the big opportunities that are ahead of you. If you keep sowing, some seeds will fall on good ground and germinate.

Ways to get seeds to Sow

There are many things you can do, and I suggest the following:

1. Recruit people who are willing to follow you or join you in your business.
2. Protect your seeds and your life.
3. You need to develop your organizational skills.
4. Communicate to people about your seeds so they can come for them.

The Purpose of Parables;
why did Jesus use Parables

And the disciples came and said to Him, "Why do you speak to them in parables?" He answered and said to them, "Because it has been given to you to know the mysteries of the kingdom of heaven, but to them, it has not been given. For whoever has, to him more will be given, and he will have abundance; but whoever does not have, even what he has will be taken away from him. Therefore I speak to them in parables, because seeing they do not see, and hearing they do not hear, nor do they understand. And in them, the prophecy of Isaiah is fulfilled, which says: 'Hearing you will hear and shall not understand, and seeing you will see and not perceive; for the hearts of this people have grown dull.Their ears are hard of hearing, and their eyes they have closed, Lest they should see with their eyes and hear with their ears, Lest they should understand with their hearts and turn, So that I should heal them.' But blessed are your eyes for they see, and your ears for they hear; for assuredly, I say to you that many prophet and righteous men desired to see what you see, and did not see it, and to hear what you hear, and did not heart. (Matthew 13:11-17)

The Parable of the Sower Explained

Therefore hear the parable of the sower: When anyone hears the word of the kingdom and does not understand it, then the wicked one comes and snatches away what was sown in his heart. This is he who received seed by the wayside. But he who received the seed on stony places, this is he who hears the word and immediately receives it with joy; yet he has no root in himself but endures only for a while. For when tribulation or persecution arises because of the word, immediately he stumbles. Now he who received seed among the thorns is he, who hears the word, and the cares of this world and the deceitfulness of riches choke the word, and he becomes unfruitful. But he who received seed on the good ground is he who hears the word and understands it, who indeed bears fruit and produces: some a hundredfold, some sixty, some thirty." (Matthew 13:18-23)

My suggestion is to teach this parable to your children, family, church or organization. In addition, apply this parable in your life. Finally, master this parables.

The Parable of the Wheat and the Tares

Another parable He put forth to them, saying: "The kingdom of heaven is like a man who sowed good seed in his field; but while men slept, his enemy came and sowed tares among the wheat and went his way. But when the grain had sprouted and produced a crop, then the tares also appeared. So the servants of the owner came and said to him, 'Sir did you not so good seed in your field? How then does it have tares?' He said to them, 'An enemy has done this.' The servants said to him, 'Do you want us then to go and gather them up?' But he said, 'No, lest while you gather up the tares, you also uproot the wheat with them. Let both grow together until the harvest and at the time of harvest I will say to the reapers, "First gather together the tares and bind them in bundles to burn them, but gather the wheat into my barn." (Matthew 13:24-30)

The Parable of the Mustard Seed

Another parable He put forth to them, saying: "The kingdom of heaven is like a mustard seed, which a man took and sowed in his field, which indeed is the least of all the seeds; but when it is grown it is greater than the herbs and becomes a tree, so that the birds of the air come and nest in its branches." (Matthew 13:31-32)

There is nothing as powerful as a seed. A seed is a tiny "object" but hidden inside is a tree, fruits and so forth. Everything in life starts as a seed, and it is your responsibility to care and protect the seed. When my son, George, was born, he was a baby; I used to keep an eye on him when he slept at night and during the day. Now that he is in high school, I speak with him. Why? He was a seed. If you are going to influence today's generation, do not wait for them to become big; start small and grow until you dominate your family or generation.

The Parable of the Leaven

Another parable He spoke to them: *"The kingdom of heaven is like leaven, which a woman took and hid in three measures of meal till it was all leavened."* (Matthew 13:33). Have you imagined what this process implies? What does it mean "All of it was leavened?" This is a powerful statement connected to the power of influence.

The Power of Prophecy and Parables

> *All these things Jesus spoke to the multitude in parables; and without a parable He did not speak to them, that it might be fulfilled which was spoken by the prophet, saying: "I will open my mouth in parables; I will utter things kept secret from the foundation of the world." There are things you have been told in parables, and until now you have not understood them. You need to take time off to reflect on those things. You need to think and interpret those things in your life. There are things that will remain a mystery to you or said in parables; it is up to you to discover and apply them in your life.* (Matthew 13:34-35)

The Parable of the Hidden Treasure

> *"Again, the kingdom of heaven is like treasure hidden in a field, which a man found and hid; and for joy over it he goes and sells all that he has and buys that field."* (Matthew 13:44)

In the ancient days of the Greeks and Romans, a treasury was a place where the riches were concentrated. Jesus said when you find the treasure, then you have the Kingdom of Heaven. For you to have influence, you need to discover the hidden treasure in your field, life or community, then go sell it and you will find buyers. The buyers are clients or customers. Most humans have not discovered the hidden treasure. The important point to remember is you need to discover the hidden treasure as a leader. The "hidden treasure" is available to anyone who asks (Matthew 7:7).

The Parable Of The Pearl Of Great Price

"Again, the kingdom of heaven is like a merchant seeking beautiful pearls, who, when he had found one pearl of great price, went and sold all that he had and bought it." (Matthew 13:45-46)

To become a person of influence, you must study this parable. It talks about a pearl of great price. A pearl is a product that is beautiful and has a high economic value. It is also the only precious gemstone that comes from a living thing, when an oyster secretes the material that forms the pearl. This reminds us that people are more precious than material things.

Something that has high economic value is rare. It is uncommon; therefore, to become an influence or great requires you to become an economic product with high value. Without value, your influence is canceled. If you keep drinking or destroying your life with bad company, you will never be a rare commodity. What treasure do you have?

I believe leaders are rejected because of their vision, proposals, convictions, actions, purpose, ideas and belief systems. It is also easier for someone to destroy than create. A person who is unwilling to pay the price for success will attempt to criticize it because they think it vindicates their apathy and laziness.

God's Strategy for Mankind on Earth

In life, you will say or do things that will offend people in your home city or country. That is natural and to be expected. You could be doing a project that benefits the community, but believe me, it will attract the attention of people who will oppose your ideas and plans. You should not give up when this happens; instead keep going and seeking advice. Jesus did not give up when His own people and one of his closest friends turned against him. He kept on going and believed in His assignments. You will reach moments in your life when you feel like quitting or giving up, but that is the moment when the season is about to turn and you will experience peace.

You must understand that:

1. God Predestined All of Us

The subject of faith is very hard to teach human being. It is very difficult to convince people to believe in something that they cannot see because humans are creatures of things which can be seen. The problem with people is they believe what they see even if it isn't true. Faith is something that is hard to teach. It is easier to attend a mass than convert a Muslim to believe Jesus Christ is the Son of God.

The reason is because people grow up believing certain things and no amount of proof or logic is going to get them to change.

If you believe that God exists and that His word is in the Holy Bible, then believe everything written in the Bible and not just parts of the Scripture. Do not be selective. Belief is faith. Faith believes in things not seen. We all believe there is a place called Heaven. That means we need to believe our destiny is in the hands of God (Ephesians 1:11).

2. Always Remember That God Predestined You

The most powerful Scripture in my life is Ephesian 1:11. *"In Him also we have obtained an inheritance, being predestined according to the purpose of Him who works all things according to the counsel of His will."* When I was a teenager in high school, this verse changed my life and helped me to navigate through the challenges of residing in a slum and going to school without basic necessities. It got into my soul and spirit. Each time I was faced with challenges and trials, I would have a positive attitude that my destiny is set or decided by God. I decided that I would always obey God's Word, so He leads me to that "predestined end." I learned that the destiny of a seed is a tree and seeds and trees and forests. The destiny of a calf is a cow and herds. God created everything to have a destiny. God's will is more important than our ideas and is more powerful than our power, plans, or thoughts. Only God can do all things according to His will.

I believe that God predestined the end of every human. God knows the end from the beginning of everything. Thus, God predestined you according to the purpose of He Who works all things according to the purpose of His will. God says all things. God works according to His purpose, not our intelligence, wisdom, power, wealth, and ideas. Therefore you need to keep your plans in line with His purpose. When we are out of God's purpose, we will not succeed and our plans will fail.

3. God Thinks in a Different Way

God says, *"My thoughts are not your thoughts neither my ways your ways."* God thinks in a way that is different from us. In other words, to become like God, we have to study His Word. When we learn His Word, they become our thoughts. When we learn God's thoughts, we begin to take on the nature of God, speak His Words, and the Words become our Words. In the same manner, when we begin to walk in God's ways, God will begin to lead us to a path of righteousness. If you follow someone, it means you are following their footsteps.

It is important to know that your destiny is chosen by God, Who predestined you before He began the foundation of the Earth. You need to think and walk in the ways of God. Let God's thoughts from His words occupy and colonize your mind, fill your mind with His words, and actualise your purpose; God's purpose will manifest.

4. God's Ultimate Purpose is Permanent

And we know that all things work together for good to those who love God, to those who are called according to His purpose. For whom He foreknew, He also predestined to be conformed to the image of His Son, that He might be the firstborn among many brethren. Moreover whom He predestined, these He also called; whom He called, these He also justified; and whom He justified, and these He also glorified. (Romans 8:28-30).

5. God Demands Love From Mankind

God wants us to love Him. Many people love God because of the good things He gave them—the blessings and gifts. We need to love God because He is God. He knows the purpose of everyone. He knew it before and destined already. This means your future is God's history. It is God's past.

The Principle of Humble Beginnings

Job 8:7 says, *"Though your beginning was small, yet your latter end would increase abundantly."* The majority of people want to become rich instantly. This is why many people, including public servants, are in prison. I believe with all my heart that God creates every human to start as small as possible before becoming big and great. God told Job that even though you are small right now, by the end of your life, you will have plenty. You will be great and you will be an influence. It is always important to remember that if you are persistent and consistent, you will never stay the same. The most important thing is to work.

Mandela National Stadium in Kampala, Uganda

One day, I was in a car washing bay in Kampala, when I saw the words printed in bold capital letters on top of the Mandela National Stadium. It occurred to me that Nelson Mandela has been dead for several years, but his name is still on the stadium. I believe this was made possible because of Mandela's life story of perseverance in the midst of persecution. Mandela spent 27 years in prison for the sake of black South Africans who were oppressed by the apartheid regime. He was first black South African President. You cannot be remembered by history unless you have a price, test or crisis that you have to overcome. Mandela will live forever and his name will be talked about for generations.

What Comes to Your Mind?

Do you think you will be remembered by history when you are gone? How will people remember you? If you want to be remembered, you have a lot of work to do, and that means making sacrifices to influence your generation. Mandela did not give up on his convictions. He was considered a terrorist for standing against what was wrong, but he did not give up until he achieved his goal of abolishing the apartheid regime.

KNOW
HOW GOD
WORKS

7

God Predestines Everything

*It is in your moments of decision
that your destiny is shaped.*
Tony Robbins

God Decides Destiny

Let me be as direct as possible. god decides the destiny and the end of things, but you must obey his laws to reach your destination. Remember also that God is always hiding big things in little things. Imagine a mango seed, hiding a mango tree. This principle is found in Genesis 1:11-12:

> Then God said, 'Let the Earth bring forth grass, the herb that yields seed, and the fruit tree that yields fruit according to its kind, whose seed is in itself, on the Earth and it was so. And the Earth brought forth grass, the herb that yields seed according to its kind, and the tree that yields fruit, whose seed is in itself according to its kind. And God saw that it was good.

Everything you wish to become in life is trapped inside of you, just like the seed that contains fruits and trees from the inside. When you decide to take the seed and plant it in good soil, you will see the process the seed takes to become a tree and reproduce trees and seeds. The destiny of the seed is already predestined by the creator. God did the same with other creatures from His creative works. He placed the future of a herd of cattle in one cow. He placed the future of humanity in two people whom he commanded to multiply and fill up the Earth.

David the Shepherd, King and Leader

David, the son of Jesse, was the youngest in the family and his main duty was to tend his father's sheep. While in the field, David encountered certain challenges he needed to overcome. The sheep were attacked by wild animals who wanted to kill the sheep. David, based on experience, was able to save the sheep by killing the wild animals like a bear and lion. This experience was very risky for these animals are very fierce, but they made David stronger in his attitude towards life. He also used to practice slinging stones.

Nobody knew David was destined to be the next king of Israel. His family members never knew that David was the next king. When King Saul failed as a leader by disobeying God, God decided to anoint another king. Prophet Samuel was asked by God to go to the house of Jesse to anoint the next king. When the prophet arrived at the house and asked for the next king to be anointed there was none because God's spirit had not shown him David. He went on to ask if the father had another son and it was then the father remembered he had another son. He brought in David who was "smelly" from working with animals. He was anointed, and the Spirit of God started to work in him.

One day, David's father sent him to take food to his brothers who were fighting God's enemies, the Philistines. When David arrived at the front lines he was surprised at what he saw. He saw the Israelites afraid of one man named Goliath. David knew he had the power and potential to kill the Philistine giant, but everyone, includng his brothers ridiculed him, saying there was no way a small kid like him could ever defeat someone so large.

David didn't care what they said, for he knew that God was with him. David used a sling to hit the forehead of Goliath with a stone, then the giant fell and David ran over to cut off his head. The moment David did that, everything changed. He became popular. What happened? A leader was born.

Moses the Prince, Deliverer and Leader of Israel

When Moses was a young boy, nobody knew that he would one day lead a big mission to deliver the Israelites. Moses was born to a Jewish woman during a time when all the boys were to be killed. The mother, through the guidance of God, decided to put the baby in a small "boat" and let him float down the Nile. The daughter of Pharaoh saw the baby and decided to adopt the child. Moses was taken from the hands of his mother and raised in the palace. Moses went to the school where the rest of Pharaoh's kids studied, which was one of the top schools in Egypt.

After completing his studies, Moses returned to the palace. One day Moses saw an Egyptian beating a Jew. He was angry to the point of committing murder. He ran away from Egypt to the wilderness. While in exile, Moses married the daughter of Jethro. He became a shepherd looking after the flock of his father-in-law. He did this for 40 years in the desert.

As a matter of fact, Exodus 3 says,

> *Now Moses was tending the flock of Jethro his father-in-law, the priest of Midian, and he led the flock to the far side of the wilderness and came to Horeb, the mountain of God. There the angel of the Lord appeared to him in flames of fire from within a bush. Moses saw that though the bush was on fire, it did not burn up. So Moses thought, "I will go over and see this strange sight—why the bush does not burn up... It was these event that resulted in Moses receiving instructions to deliver Israel. You should never write people off.*

God's Purposes is More Important than Man's Plans

A lot of people never pursue their leadership visions because of their past deeds and experiences. They are held back because of their failures or successes. Your leadership does not have to be held by your personal failures, successes or circumstances that you cannot change or control. For that, it does not matter what you have done in life. What matters is God's instructions and purpose. If God has purposed you to be somebody, it will happen because God's purposes are permament. For instance, Moses was a fugitive and a murderer. He was in exile for many years in the desert of Sinai until that day when God gave him responsibility and the assignment of delivering his people from oppression and leading them to the Promised Land.

You might be wondering what your assignment is in the world. I want to encourage you, your appointment or information about your assignment is coming. The news is going to reach you. Those who have been laughing at you are going to think twice. The truth of the matter is that Moses' future destiny in leadership was trapped inside, waiting for the right time to burst forth. Moses went beyond being a leader to being a judge, and an author. Moses is known as the writer of Genesis, Exodus, Numbers, Leviticus and Deuteronomy.

As a young man, Moses never knew that God would use him to write books. I believe the reason God allowed Moses to be raised in Pharaoh's palace and attend school was to prepare him for his assignments. There are things you are going through right now that look hopeless or useless. But believe me, there is something God is preparing for you after that experience.

Every experience or situation in life has something to teach humanity. Imagine the work of a shepherd in the wilderness. Moses was being prepared to lead the people just as he took care of his father-in-law's sheep. If Moses had not gotten that experience in the wilderness, maybe he would not have managed to lead the people.

Furthermore, by living in the desert, Moses gained experience of the challenges of life in the desert. When Moses succeeded in getting the people of Israel released, he had to lead them through the same place he had spent 40 years as a shepherd.

However, his brother Aaron was not in the desert. His friend Joshua joined him later. Moses' situation could be similar to what you are going through right now. You might be in the wilderness alone, without family or friends. God is saying, "Hang in there." Do not give up. It will bring you out stronger than when you went into that situation. When you come out, God will also bring an Aaron or Joshua to work with you to fulfill the mission. Stay steady. Be focused and have personal discipline. Only God knew the destiny of Moses and the things he would accomplish.

Joshua, the Follower of Moses Installed as Leader

When Moses, died, God said to Josua that Moses is dead. I believe He said, there is no other leader. You have to become one and lead the people since you have been with Moses. The whole story is in Joshua 1:1-19. There are so many promises that God made to Joshua which are:

1. God told Joshua and the people to get ready to take over the Promised Land.
2. God promised that every place they set their feet will be their land.
3. God described the size of the area that they will own.
4. God promised to stand by Joshua's side and that nobody would sucessfully stand against him.
5. God promised never to forsake Joshua.
6. God told Joshua to be strong and courageous.
7. God told Joshua to obey all the laws to be successful. You too can be successful if you learn to obey the laws of God.
8. God commanded the Isrealites to meditate on the law during day and night and be careful to obey everything written in it.
9. God said the final result of obedience to his laws is that there will be prosperity and successful life and living.

The point of the above examples is to demonstrate that nobody knows what you are destined to be or do in life. My life is a testimony to the work of God. I was born in a rural community and raised in a poor neighborhood. Everyone around our family was rich by societal standards. In those days, if a family had a large herd of cows, they were considered wealthy and successful. When I was entering high school, my father had to sell cows to pay for my tuition. The wealthy families had many cows but very few would be willing to sell for their children to go to school. My father was always willing to give his best and support for us to go to school. Through the support of relatives and my dad, I was able, by God's grace, to complete my university education. I became the first person in my family to graduate from the Makerere University. For example, I am also the first PhD holder in my community and possibly among the few in the entire district of Bukedea. God knows the destiny of everything.

Are Leaders Born or Made?

There has been a lot of debate on whether leaders are born or made. All human beings are born naturally. Every human being comes to the world through birth. Some people get in good environments and others in bad enviromnents. Some people are born into rich or poor families. Some people go to the top schools or universities while others do not. Some people are born in rich or poor nations. Some people get opportunities and others do not.

When you study the examples of Moses and Joshua, you will realize that they became leaders because of God's plan and their experiences. Moses grew up in the palace, might have gone to best schools and got exposed to new ideas on leadership. He also was in a desert tending sheep. He might have also learned practical lessons required for leadership. For instance, he might have learned the value of patience, justice, fairness, courage, love, faith, self-discipline, endurance, obedience, submission and many more essential qualities of true leaders. He might have also matured and developed a sense of responsibility and gained a sense of meaning.

Turning to the life of Joshua, he too learned from Moses who was the leader. He was guided and participated in decision making or meetings. He was exposed to various tasks and assignments. He was taught and mentored.

1. To become a leader, you must have the attributes presented here as well as the following discoveries:
2. A leader is born when a person discovers their gift, abilities and potential.
3. A leader is born when a person solves a problem that others have failed to fix.
4. A leader always carries their leadership inside of them which is released through self-discovery.
5. A leader is always motivated to solve a problem or meet a need in the community.
6. A leader always carries his or her gift with them and sometimes, they do not know of their abilities and gifts until they discover them. I had no idea of being an author or leader until I discovered I coud actually share my ideas in a book. You have that capacity too.

Think about these statements and reflect on them carefully.

8

Believe You Are a Leader

In Him we were also chosen,
having been predestined according
to the plan of him who works out everything
in conformity with the purpose of his will.
Ephesians 1:11

God's Mandate of Dominion

When God created man, He made a statement that I believe most people do not fully understand. Genesis 1:26-28 says,

> *Then God said, 'Let Us make man in Our image, according to Our likeness; let them have dominion over the fish of the sea, over the birds of the air, and over the cattle, over all the Earth and over every creeping thing that creeps on the Earth.' So God created man in His image; in the image of God He created him; male and female He created them. Then God blessed them, and God said to them, "Be fruitful and multiply; fill the Earth and subdue it; have dominion over the fish of the sea, over the birds of the air, and over every living thing that moves on the Earth.*

135

God said let man have dominion over the all creatures in the sea, air and on Earth.

Principles of Man's Creation

1. Man was created to dominate the Earth, not individuals or people.
2. Man was designed to dominate using his God-given gifts.
3. Man's leadership mandate comes from the gift.
4. Man was created by God and has the same component as the Creator.
5. Man was not created to dominate other men or women.

The word "dominion" also means rule, authority, the sphere of influence, or the area of control. It also means to lead and manage.

Why did God Create the Heavens and Earth?

Heaven is an invisible country where the King, our God, has His throne. God lives in eternity. He created the man and put the man on the Earth in a place called the Garden of Eden. But look at what God said in Genesis 1:26-28. God said, let us make man in Our image and let him have dominion. Our reason for existence on Earth is to dominate and influence. That is why every human being was created to govern. The reason people rebel or fight against oppression is because of this gift of dominion.

When I was a pupil in primary school, I was taught that Uganda obtained its independence from Great Britain on October 9, 1962. The independence was a result of colonization. I learned that colonization refers to another government controlling or ruling another territory. The colony is always far from the colonizer. We were taught that the representative of Kingdom of Great Britain was a governor who ruled the colony. God created man to govern the colony called Earth. Because God is King, He wanted man to be a king on Earth but not over the people.

God Directed Man to Do The Following:

1. **Be fruitful:** This means that man has a seed. You cannot get fruit unless there is a seed inside the man. Every man comes to the planet with seeds. It is the seeds, when planted, that make the man fruitful. However, most human beings never take the time to plant their seeds and impact the world.

2. **Multiply:** I believe God, said, multiply the fruit. If you have seeds, you can get fruit, but all fruits have seeds inside. Therefore, man was required to multiply the fruits and seeds. A person without the capacity to multiply their seeds or fruits will have no influence.

3. **Fill the Earth:** Filling the Earth means filling it with our seeds and fruits.

4. **Subdue the Earth:** Nobody has the capacity to subdue the Earth or control it. However, man can subdue what they produce and multiply.

5. **Have dominion:** This is over everything, which includes living things, but not over other men.

Strategy for Finding your Area of Influence

When I was a young teenager, I found an interesting discovery in Genesis 1:11: *"Then God said, 'Let the land produce vegetation: seed-bearing plants and trees on the land that bear fruit with seed in it, according to their various kinds.' And it was so."* I believe with all my heart that God created everyone with seeds. A seed will always bring forth life.

Let us take an example of a mango seed. A mango seed, if placed in a right environment, will bring forth a tree, and that tree will bring forth fruit. When it produces fruit, the tree is successful. I believe the same is true with your life.

What type of tree are you?

What are the Components of a Tree?

A tree has the following elements:

1. Roots

Every tree has roots that go deep into the soil. A tree with deep roots will stand firm when the storms attack it. The opposite is also true, a tree with shallow roots will fall quickly at the least sign of resistance. The roots are symbolic of a foundation composed of the blocks used in building the tree. The roots pull the food nutrients and minerals the tree needs for survival.

One of the facts about trees is that when a seed starts to germinate, the roots will go down into the soil and later appear on the top. I believe every human being's life is like the root system. To me, the roots are composed of belief systems and convictions. I also believe that the faith a person has gives them the power to overcome any challenge or survive the storms. When a person has strong belief systems and convictions, it is not easy to kill that person.

How deep are your roots?

Dr. Martin Luther King Jr.

When I went to Atlanta, Georgia, I visited the birthplace of Dr. Martin Luther King Jr. I also visited the Ebenezer Baptist Church where his father and grandfather were both ministers. I realized that Dr. King's strength was not in himself, but he got a firm foundation from growing up in a church environment and following in the footsteps of his father and grandfather.

I believe that a person whose life has weak belief systems or weak faith cannot sustain attacks or pressure. Instead those weakened systerms will collapse under the weight of fear. True leaders have strong belief systems and convictions. They are willing to die for what they believe. You can study the examples of Nelson Mandela, Martin Luther King Jr., Abraham Lincoln and others. Aspiring leaders must study and learn something positive from real leaders.

2. Trunk

The trunk describes the purpose of the tree. The size of trunk matters because it also shows how much weight it can sustain or how many branches will emerge from the trunk. The change in the weather or seasons does not change the characteristics of the trunk. The trunk keeps growing or expanding in size. I believe the trunk determines where the tree will end up regarding manifesting branches, fruits, and leaves. A human being must know their trunk, their purpose and desired destiny or destination. Your purpose and destination in life must be clear and remain permanent.

In my book, *Success Principles*, I wrote extensively on keys and principles of purpose. God's Word in Proverbs 19:21

proclaims, *"Many are the plans in a man's heart, but it is the Lord's purpose that prevails."* God's purpose is more important than your plans. Purpose gives stability and should never change. When you know your purpose, you have a stable life. You are fixed and never moved by the winds of life or various seasons that occur. Leaders must know their purpose and pursue it. Regardless of the attacks on the trunk, the tree will remain steady because of the power of the roots, belief systems and convictions.

Do you know your life's purpose?

3. Branches

The branches of the tree emerge from the trunk and expand the size of the tree. The branches are connected to leaves and fruits. Every tree has its gifts that it delivers. The same is true with every human being. Every human being is unique because of their gifts, skills, abilities, traits, temperaments, and talents. It is these unique attributes that separate every individual from another and lead us to our destination and fulfilment of purpose. The purpose of the tree is to bring forth fruits. If a seed does not produce seeds and fruits, that seed is a failure.

For a tree to produce fruits, the roots must do their job of bringing nutrients and minerals to the rest of the tree. Your belief systems and faith are essential elements if the fruits are to be manifested.

Do you know your gifts, skills, abilities, and talents?

4. Fruit

The fruits cannot come from the branches. Every seed must produce more seeds. A mango seed must produce mango trees and fruits. The goal of having seeds is to produce seeds, trees, and fruits. When you have used your gifts, talents, abilities and skills, you will accomplish certain things. I believe every human being was created to produce fruit. I believe fruits might mean hospitals, schools, houses for orphans or books. I also believe fruits are visions that benefit humanity or goals that are implemented to solve human problems. I also think of many things such as companies, products, services or firms that help people. What kind of fruits have you been producing?

5. Leaves

Leaves always have a unique appearance and do a lot of things. Scientists say they manufacture food. I also know that leaves give shade. The problem with leaves is eventually they fall off or change color. I believe that every human being has things that need to be put aside, kept away or even discarded because they are no longer necessary and sometimes keep people away from big things. These things, at times, are not significant. Cars, iPads, iPods, phones, etc., are good, but sometimes they are like leaves that need to be brushed aside.

When there is a change in weather, the leaves will fall off. Leaves will always fall away, and so it is with all the beautiful accumulated things in life. The storms in life could be restructuring, the death of a spouse, loss of vision, loss of foresight, family disagreements, bad investment decisions, or things that affect you severely.

Human being or an aspiring leader must have strong roots or strong foundation. They must know their purpose and destiny. They must have branches and bring forth fruits, but they need to know that people come to them not because they know their purpose but because of fruits. Also, leaders need to know that leaves can fall off the tree, and that must be expected because of changing weather patterns or climatic conditions.

Principles and Takeaways

1. Every follower is capable of leadership.
2. Every follower has the capacity to lead and be a leader.
3. All human beings were created to lead and dominate.
4. All people have the potential to manifest leadership.
5. The destiny of a seed is a tree and fruits.
6. Every follower is destined for leadership.
7. Every seed goes through a process to become a tree and produce fruits.
8. Every person must go through a process to become the leader they were designed to be.
9. Every person must go through training, development, learning, experiences, setbacks, challenges, assessments, tests and mentoring.

What is True Leadership?

I believe that there is confusion regarding the term leadership. When I enrolled in a graduate school at Uganda Christian University, I studied leadership and management of organization. The concept of leadership was re-introduced into my life from the Biblical and secular viewpoints. During my first semester at Regent University, we were required to study leadership theories, leaders and followers.

There were different explanations regarding leadership. What leaders do and why they do it. As a student of leadership, I studied the different theories, strengths and weaknesses of each theory and its application. During that time, I developed my own conclusions about leadership which I am pleased to share with you:

1. Leadership does not mean dictating over other people.
2. Leadership is not about intimidating others. Instead, leadership is about inspiring followers.
3. Leadership does not mean controlling people. Humans beings are complicated; you cannot control them.
4. Leadership does not manipulate or manage people. Rather, leadership motivates them to achieve their highest potential.
5. Leadership does not mean ruling people. Leadership is about serving the people.
6. Leadership is not about being served. Rather, leadership is serving others through inherent gifts.
7. Leadership does not mean harassing others. Again, it is about serving them.
8. Leadership is not about using power. Leadership is about empowers people.
9. Leadership is not about using and abusing power. Leadership upholds correct principles and values.
10. Leadership is not about pursuing people. Instead, leadership is about pursuing purpose.
11. Leadership is not about manipulating followers. Instead, it is about mentoring followers.

Think of what your leaders do in connection to the statements above.

Do We Really Have True Leaders?

In my view, we have very few true leaders. Most of the leaders the world has produced are not really "true leaders." If you are a leader, you need to check to see if you are doing any of the above. The reason people who are oppressed fight for their independence is because humans do not want to be controlled, manipulated, or ruled. They want to be in charge, rule, control and dominate. This simply means that they have the capacity to dominate.

When God created humans, He also placed in them the ability to perform. God placed the law of potential in everything he created. When God told Abraham that His descendants would be innumerable, He gave Abraham the capacity to bring it to pass. When God called Moses to become the leader of his oppressed people in Egypt, God provided what was needed for leadership. He provided resources and a spokesman, his brother Aaron. Therefore, we can say that whatever God calls He provides and makes provision.

All human are created with the capacity to lead. This is why life passes through stages such as infancy, childhood, adolescence and adulthood. Once the process is completed, they will become leaders. The value of a thing is not determined by the opinions of people but the degree to which the product is considered rare or scarce. The more valuable a person becomes, the more value they attract.

What kind of leader are you in relations to statements on page 125?

9

Leadership Comes At a Cost

The price of greatness is responsibility.
Winston Churchill

Tests That Leaders Must Face in Leadership Position

True leaders are never remembered by their medals. Instead, they are remembered by the price they paid at the end of their lives. The people to trust are those with battle scars, not those who are good at talking. Have you survived from some experience in life? The pursuit of leadership will cost any person who comes forward to lead others. If you are going to take a leadership position, you will need to get ready for some of the following tests and costs that will come your way:

1. Self-Sacrifice

There will always come a time when a leader will have to sacrifice for the sake of his followers. Jesus Christ sacrificed himself on the cross. He had to pay the price for us, and through His sacrifice, we obtained salvation. In my own life,

I sacrificed many things in my youth so my siblings could get educated. Today, out of the five kids, four of us have gone through university education. This came from self-sacrifice and foregoing the pleasures of life. The freedom in my country was bought at a high price; my President himself was almost killed during the Bush war.

2. Rejection

When a leader steps forward, he will immediately find that he has enemies. Jesus Christ was an unknown young man, just the son of Joseph and Mary. He, too, was their son, not only God's. But when he began to speak and tell the people to repent, the Pharisees and Sadducees rejected His philosophy, views, vision and ideas. You might have great ideas that can improve society, but rest assured, you will also face rejection. Sometimes even members of your own household might not agree with you.

3. Criticisms

This is very common for all those who usually come forward to lead. The leader might have ideas that people will attack. They might be criticized for taking a position that is outside the mainstream.

4. Attacks

The story of Jospeh in the Bible comes to mind here; his brothers threw him into the pit and sold him to the slave masters in Egypt. Leaders will always come under attack. Mandela and John. F. Kennedy are just a couple of examples of leaders who were attacked.

5. Loss of Life

In some cases, leaders might even lose their lives. Examples include Stephen, who was chosen in Acts 5, but paid the price of leadership in the early church. Another example is Dr. Martin Lurther King Jr., a Civil Rights leader in the US, who lost his life when he was gunned down for fighting for justice, equality and freedom. There are many more examples of leaders who paid the untimate price for their convictions.

6. Loneliness

In many cases, leaders will find themselves being lonely. There are examples of Moses in the desert, Jesus in the wilderness, and David looking after the sheep. If you are unwilling to be alone, then do not pursue leadership. My experience of living in Somalia and Nigeria is that most times I wanted to give up and quit the mission. But each morning, my purpose motivats me to keep going in the midst challenges. My personal purpose is to equip and empower aspiring leaders to serve humanity. Ecclesiastes 3:1 kept me going. It says, *"there is time for everything, a time for every purpose under heaven."*

7. Peer Pressure

Leaders will find themselves coming under intense peer pressure. They will be tempted to obtain things that are not right or offer favors to those closest to them. Jesus Christ experienced pressure from the mother of James and John (Matthew 20: 21).

8. Fatigue

Leadership is exhausting: mentally, physically, spiritually and financially. A lot is expected from the leader by the followers. As revealed in the Bible, that is why Jesus Christ sometimes hides from His followers. You can check the story in John 6. Jesus had to go away for a while from the members who wanted Him to solve their problems or meet their needs.

9. Relationship Mishaps

Leaders have trusted members and enemies. There will be those who believe in the leader, but others will doubt. Peter believed in Jesus. Thomas doubted Him. Judas decided to betray Him. He conspired with the Pharisees and Sadducees to have Jesus killed.

10. Betrayed or Betrayal

Leaders also face the risk of betrayal. A leader attracts followers, but sometimes the followers can turn and betray the leader. In Matthew 26:23-25, Jesus was betrayed by Judas and denied three times by his best friend, Peter. If you read the earlier verses, you will find where it says Judas agreed to betray Jesus and asked to be paid money.

Leaders Paid the Price for Leadership

Jesus, whom I believe was the ultimate leader, did many great things. He healed the sick, blind, raised Lazarus from the grave, provided 5,000 men with food, and gave people wine during the wedding party. Jesus did many good things, but at the end, He paid the price with His own life. Even one of the closest friends, Peter, said when the going got rough, *"I do not know that man Jesus"* (Matthew 26:69-74).

One thing that is interesting about Jesus is that regardless of what came His way, he continued with what He came to do. When His friends turned against Him, He gladly paid the price. Judas received money but eventually committed suicide. I believe that Judas lost his life because he lost his faith and not even money could save him. Even in today's world, people might have betrayed you. Accept the price and keep going. God is waiting to receive and reward you. The name of Jesus will forever be spoken because of the good things that he accomplished.

If you as a leader in your community, society or nation continue to do good things, it will be difficult to erase your works in the minds of those who turn against you. History does not remember leaders who surrender, but remembers those who paid the price. In our world, we hear names like Mahatma Gandhi (India), Martin Luther King Jr. (USA), Nelson Mandela (South Africa), Abraham Lincoln (USA), and Ignatius Musaazi (Uganda).

Wrong Motives

There are some people who want leadership positions for the wrong reasons. During Jesus' time on Earth, two brothers and their mother approached him for jobs. The story is presented in Jesus said, "...And whoever desires to be first among you, let him be your slave— just as the Son of Man did not come to be served, but to serve, and to give His life a ransom for many" (Matthew 20: 20-28).

In the passage in Matthew 20, there is a parent going to meet the leader of a prestigious organization. The mother comes with her two sons, John and James. The mother asks Jesus, the leader, for a favor. She asked Jesus to please allow her children to sit next to Him in his government. They wanted top leadership positions. You can have your interpretations of the story, but I believe they wanted superiority over the others.

Parents want their children to become great. They will do anything for their kids. You will find leaders giving their relatives or close friends positions for which they do not qualify. Can you imagine if Jesus had granted her wish?

The lesson here is that leaders must be careful of the favors some of their followers ask. There is nothing wrong in seeking favor or help, but the motives must be right and correct. Jesus explained to the young men why He could not give them the desires of their hearts (Matthew 20:23). There are some leadership positions that only God can grant.

Jesus emphasized that true greatness only come from servanthood. Indeed, if you desire clout or influence, you must become a servant. To drive home His points, Jesus said even he was serving others and not waiting to be served. Unfortunately, this is in contrast to what is obtainable in our world today as many of the people seeking leadership positions are waiting to be served but not serving others. Jesus taught that anyone wishing to take a leadership position must be willing to pay the price. Most of us think leadership is easy, but the truth is that it comes with a heavy price.

While Jesus grew up in Nazareth, nobody cared about what He was doing in the carpentry workshop with His father, Joseph. The trouble started when He began telling people to repent and called them to follow Him. Even those who never bothered Him when He was in the carpenter shop saw Him as an enemy. I recall growing up in a poor neighborhood in my village. I was nobody, but once I started to help my people and seek to the advancement of the community to help kids go to school, I became an enemy to some people.

It is imperative to know that the moment you start doing something in this world, you need to get ready for tests.

I spent my younger years working hard in hazardous areas around the world, sending money to my family and friends for upkeep, feeding, rent, school tuition, transport, medical, etc. But believe me, everyone turned and left me alone. It was hurting me, but I had to start life all over again. A home that used to be full of people at night, day, lunch or dinner, suddenly became a home of a few people. I was the leader, and I shared my ideas, ministering, taking people to church every Sunday and guiding them, but I became the enemy. Life is a teacher. I never stopped learning; I kept on working and growing myself. Any regrets? No!

James was killed by Herod (Acts 12:1-2) while John died in exile. Whatever you ask might be given to you. John and James asked Jesus about leadership role. They even said they were able to drink the cup that Jesus was about to drink before His crucifixion. The two brothers paid the price.

Some Questions for Reflection
1. What price are you willing to pay?
2. Are you willing to lose your life?
3. Have you thought about what you will do to lead your community?
4. Do you merely want to enjoy life and party nonstop?

Think about how you will be remembered. We cannot forget the lives of Peter, Stephen, John, James, and others who gave all to give us the gospel today. Jesus said if you lay down your life you will save it.

The Story of Martin Luther King Jr.

During one of my classes at the doctoral level, I studied a course called Leadership Communications; our professor asked us to study the *"I Have a Dream"* speech of Martin Luther King Jr. The speech was delivered on April 3, 1968. When Dr. King gave that speech, he knew that some of the people were not happy with him and he was prepared to pay the price. He was killed. Today, Americans continue to celebrate the life of a man who gave his own life for the freedom of others. He is celebrated annually in the US. He will forever be remembered for the courage to stand in the midst of trials and danger.

Are you willing to pay the price? As for me, I am on the course. I am pursuing what God created me to do. I am willing to pay the price. May God bless you as you do the same.

10

Understand That Leadership Is Inherent

The key to successful leadership today
is influence, not authority.
Kenneth Blanchard

Education Does Not Give You Everything

During my early years, I lived with my grandparents, who used to carry out subsistence farming. They gave pieces of land to me and each of my siblings to plant groundnuts. As a child, I used to wonder when the planting time was ready. They would give each child a certain quantity of groundnuts to plant, but during the harvest time, the amount collected was much greater than the number of seeds planted. I learned that seeds carry seeds and we were taught not to waste or destroy seeds.

These were critical and practical lessons for me as a teenager. Even in my adult life, I still apply those lessons. The principle to remember is that God places inside of every seed a seed. If you have a mango seed, and plant it, it will become a giant tree that produces large mangoes or smaller ones. The same is true with people. Sometimes, God gives us dreams or visions, but we end up creating small or big ones. There are many lessons here from (Matthew 20: 23-28).

I invite you to consider the Scriptures carefully. Jesus said He was not responsible for the two spots — sitting on the right or left in the kingdom. Jesus knew it was God's responsibility and authority. In my short journey on the planet, I believe that God decides what happens to us if we obey His laws. But if we disregard those laws, we will miss what He prepares for us. He says His purpose will prevail even though you might have your plans, ideas or strategies (Proverbs 19:21).

Delivering God's Purpose Requires Wisdom

Each person created by God has a reason why they exist. People came to Earth to accomplish that single purpose. They are created in God's image with the capacity to do what they are meant to do. You might not know your reason for existence on Earth, but with prayer, meditation, and seeking God, He will lead you. God will lead you or speak to you so you can follow your purpose.

However, prayer alone might not help you. You will need wisdom. King Solomon says every man or woman needs understanding and wisdom. Proverbs 20:5 says these words: "Counsel in the heart of man is like deep water, but a man of understanding will draw it out." Many people never strive for knowledge. They never care to buy books, preferring to purchase alcohol. They go to discos or night clubs. They think of smoking cigarettes on a Sunday morning while perusing through their girlfriends' messages in evening time.

To exploit and pursue your purpose, I believe God wants us to follow Him. We must make God our top priority. We must have

God at the center of what we do. Jesus said it in such a powerful way. Matthew 6:33-34 says, *"But seek first the kingdom of God and His righteousness, and all these things shall be added to you."* Therefore do not worry about tomorrow, for tomorrow will worry about its things. Sufficient for the day is its trouble." If you seek God, you will find Him. Our priority must be seeking God's kingdom and His righteousness. Righteousness means being in line with God's laws. If we have broken or disobeyed God's laws, we need to repent and ask for forgiveness.

The Power of Renewing the Mind

Another challenge is people continuing with old information or an outdated mentality. The knowledge you acquired several years ago might not be relevant today. You need to purge old information from the subconscious mind. You need to plant new seeds of information to advance ahead of life. Paul, a great apostle of Jesus Christ, said these words to the Romans: *"And do not be conformed to this world, but be transformed by the renewing of your mind, that you may prove what is that good and acceptable and perfect will of God"* (Romans 12:2). Paul said that transformation only occurs when the mind gets renewed.

The human mind is a storehouse of information. Whatever is received is stored in the mind. Even pictures or movies get stored. The mind is a powererful tool that God gave you, and if you want to change your life, it must be renewed. Renewal requires you to allow only useful information or ideas to be stored while rejecting others.

The renewal of the mind is the most important act you can do in your lifetime. Renewal of the mind will cause you to think differently, which leads to transformation, which leads to changes in your life and how you perceive and view life, issues, problems or opportunities.

Worries Have Destroyed Millions of People

Have you known some individuals who have lost their life because of worries? Jesus Christ counseled the disciples with a very powerful message about problems. He asked a question that I believe the disciples never answered:

Then He said to His disciples, *"Therefore I say to you, do not worry about your life, what you will eat; nor about the body, what you will put on. Life is more than food, and the body is more than clothing. Consider the ravens, for they neither sow nor reap, which have neither storehouse nor barn; and God feeds them. Of how much more value are you than the birds? And which of you by worrying can add one cubit to his stature? If you then are not able to do the least, why are you anxious for the rest? Consider the lilies, how they grow: they neither toil nor spin; and yet I say to you, even Solomon in all his glory was not arrayed like one of these. If then God so clothes the grass, which today is in the field and tomorrow is thrown into the oven, how much more will He clothe you, O you of little faith?* (Luke 12:25-28)

God can provide and meet our daily needs. A lot of people worry about what they will eat, wear, or where to sleep. If you are going to be a leader, you need to stop worrying. You need to develop to a level where your daily needs are no longer as important as what God created you to do. The quantity of your faith is directly related to what you expect in life. According to Jesus, the disciples were worried about food, clothes, and any other things because they had little faith.

Every Day Potential is Buried in Graveyards

I recall attending the funeral of a young man who was my agemate at the time of his death. This young man was academically gifted. He had great brains and was good at mathematics. Years later, I thought about him when I saw some of our classmates after they completed their college education, starting their families, having their kids, and taking senior leadership positions in government. I thought to myself, if my friend had lived, where would he be today? What position of leadership would he be holding?

I understood early in life that death is for everyone, whether you are poor or rich, educated or ignorant. In fact, there is only one person who never experienced death according to the Bible; his name was Enoch. A person who died and rose again is my personal Savior, Jesus Christ. This means death is not something to dread but something to rejoice over. The worst thing in life is the burial of potential. I remember one of my close friends- Robert. He was very bright and exceptional. He lost his life at a young age and went to his grave with all of his gifts, potential, ideas, plans, and treasure. He was never able to share them with humanity. My friend died young, and today we still miss the leadership he could have offered. If you are 30, 40, 50 or 60 years old today, are you realizing the potential you are carrying? What a tragedy. Our graveyards are filled up with great men and women who died poor, miserable, and lived wasted lives.

Do You Believe You Have Potential?

If you do not believe you can do something great let me say that you have potential. The potential is the ability you have not used. The potential is gifts or talents not yet utilized. The potential is the degree that you can get, but you have not registered for a course. The potential is the farm you have been thinking about buying, but nobody has seen. Potential is the ideas you are thinking about but never get implemented. Potential is a vision inside of you that never gets pursued or the dreams that you are carrying on a daily basis.

In Genesis, God told Adam to name all the animals. How could God ask an uneducated man to give each creature a specific name? It is also worth noting that God did this "to see what he would call them." This shows that the Creator of the universe is curious about something we do that is insignificant, relatively speaking. The wording suggests that God really wanted to know why Adam called a giraffe a giraffe, a dog a dog and so on. God is very personable and cares about even the littlest things in our lives.

I never thought I could write a book. But when I started my doctoral studies, I was taught the various professional writing styles. I studied how God's Word was written. The Bible says it was written through the inspiration of the Holy Spirit. Then I decided that if God inspires me to write, I will do it. You are reading a book that would have been buried with me if I had not followed through on my gift. Future generations of kids would have been robbed of the wisdom and ideas contained in this book.

The Origin of Potential Concept

Genesis 1 gives the account of creation. It reveals how God created everything, the heavens and Earth. Where was everything created? God was carrying everything inside Him. When God decided what He wanted to see happen, He began to work. Without work, it is impossible to manifest your potential. If you want to produce a product, you will need to sit down and work on the idea. When you choose to do what needs to be done, you will produce the product.

People's Judgment and Condemnation in Our World

You might have been judged as a failure by others. People might know and be unwilling to forget the bad things you did years ago, and they are holding that against you. Let me tell you; you have potential that nobody knows except you and God.

Let's look at the life of Joshua. Did Joshua know he was going to be the next leader? No. It wasn't until just before Moses died that he was chosen to become the next leader. Only God knew the leadership potential Joshua was carrying.

Moses murdered an Egyptian and ran away, but he is known as the writer of the first five books of the Bible. Some people have said that your ideas or dreams will never become a reality. They have never believed in you, but do not worry about them. Only God knows what he placed inside of you.

God never throws away people. He uses our mess and lets the mess become a miracle. He uses our tests to become a testimony for His greatness and glory. Saul was a murderer, but God used him as a leader. Acts 6 talks about what Saul (or Paul later) was doing when Stephen was stoned to death. But God used Paul to preach the good news of the kingdom more than those who were considered "holy."

God is about to do things in your life that will shock people. God uses the people least expected to do great things. God used Paul as an apostle to witness about His kingdom and to witness to the Gentiles throughout the Roman Empire, including Spain and England.

Our Desires and Dreams

I was traveling to the airport in Abuja, the Nigerian Capital City, when a driver told me a story about the city. He said Lagos was the first capital of Nigeria. In the early 1990s, President Ibrahim Babangida announced that the capital would be built at the center of the country. As I thought about this, I wondered if this was his dream or desire. Only God knows. I believe that we all have desires, along with genuine and false dreams. Our dreams get buried during the early years of our lives when our parents destroy them by their negative words or comments. Every parent needs to allow their kids to pursue their desires or dreams.

If someone wants to lead, let them pursue it because their capacity is built inside. If someone intends to open a business, let them pursue it. If someone loves to be a musician, let them go for it. Ephesians 2:10 says, *"For we are His workmanship, created in Christ Jesus for good works, which God prepared beforehand that we should walk in them."* We are designed to carry out good works, which only God made in advance. If what a person is pursuing does not destroy or harm others, then it is God's plan and arrangement.

My final thoughts are that you have an inherent ability to lead, but you must develop your leadership and exploit your potential. You must also believe, that you are inherently a leader. Nobody will give you leadership, you are already born with that leadership ability. The only problem, you are not a leader yet is because, you have not discovered your gift, your education has mislead you and you might have been affected by culture, bad environment and wrong association. Further, you might have been receiving wrong knowledge and information.

Think about those issues.

11

Share Your Gift And Potential

The greatest gift that you can give
to othersis the gift of unconditional
love and acceptance.
Brian Tracy

Leadership Involves Loving Your Neighbour

Leadership is love. Luke 10:27 says,

So he answered and said, "You shall love the LORD your God with all your heart, with all your soul, with all your strength, and with all your mind, and your neighbour as yourself.' And He said to him, You have answered rightly; do this and you will live.

When Jesus sent His disciples (whom I also refer to as "leadership interns") into the community, he gave them instructions about who to love and the way to love. He commanded them to love God. He did not stop there. He continued with the phrase, "with all your heart, strength and mind" and also love "your neighbors as yourself." A leader who does not love people will mistreat and manipulate them. He will use the people to achieve his political ambitions and power. A corrupt leader will also exploit the followers and does not care about them at all.

I am the first child in a family of 11 siblings. I recall years when I started to take on leadership functions by looking after my siblings. I had to offer advice, direction and motivation. I used to provide them with basic needs and share everything that I was able to get. I was a leader.

Without love, I would not have done that. Leadership is love. You cannot lead people that you do not love. Leaders must love before they lead, but sometimes people are not easy to love. Leaders cannot lead if they do not value other human beings. Valuing people comes from the recognition that they are created in God's image.

Jesus taught about love to the disciples, who were His leadership students. If a person aspires to become a leader, he or she must have a genuine love of the people he or she leads. A lot of individuals want to lead without having true love for those who follow them. A leader must love the followers and be willing to sacrifice for their good. In addition, to become a leader you must be like the little children. The story of Jesus and little children is found in Matthew 19:13-21.

You might want to study the text above in detail, but I will explain two things. First, Jesus loved the children. When the disciples tried to stop them, He told them the kingdom of God belongs to kids, not adults. He further went on to say that unless one become like children in obedience and simple act of faith, it will be hard to inherit the kingdom of God.

The Leadership Questions:

- What kind of leader are you?
- Do you love children?
- Are you concerned about their future?
- What kind of future do you think the children will inherit?
- Do you love people?
- What actions are you currently takingas a leader that has disastrous consequences for future generations?
- Will the next generation appreciate your efforts?
- Will they celebrate your life because of your deeds?

You might be wondering why these Chapter is too short. It is deliberately prepared in that way. If you are really serious about understanding the concept of potential, I would like you to get a copy of my book on *Success Principles*. In that book, I have a Chapter dedicated on the concept of potential. Potential is one of the fundamental principles for success in everything.

Everyone has potential. A seed has potential to produce seeds, fruits and fruits. The same is with you. You have the potential to become a leader. You can lead and you can achieve greatness. You can achieve your goals and dreams. The power is inside you. That power is known as potential.

Do you believe that you have potential? You have. It is trapped inside you. Believe that you have the potential. You need to cultivate, feed, release and exploit it.

Let me share with you a brief story. I was a victim of people's opinion and wrong ideas about myself when I was a teenager, until I discoverdd that I was born with potential based on the seed principle and ideas about me being created in God's image. Ephesians 3: 20 says, *"Now to Him who is able to do exceedingly abundantly above all that we ask or think, according to the power that works in us."* The power is inside you. That power is potential.

12

Be Yourself

When Jesus spoke again to the people,
he said, "I am the light of the world.
Whoever follows me will never walk in darkness,
but will have the light of life.
John 8:12

Being Yourself is key in Successful Living and Leadership

A lot of people are afraid of being themselves. I have met individuals who accumulated wealth and still felt insecure about their future. For over 15 years since I left college, I have spent most of my time serving in different positions and organizations to help the needy and vulnerable people. I have worked in war-ravaged areas, and the lessons I learned have shaped my thinking. I have worked with organizations that target the poor, and it was a great privilege to serve them. I recall watching three families three families who had returned from Cameroon in Mubi's local government. These three families with kids had hope in their eyes but had no property. The husband of one of the women said, "We believe in our ability to get back on our feet again." This is instructive because he had belief in himself.

During those moments, the little contribution I made was felt by those I met at work. I noticed that many times when I helped people. For instance, helping a poor old woman get food at a distribution point, it was more fulfilling than anything I had done. It was also gratifying to help malnourished children receive nutritional food and then later see how much they improved.

I also recall working for World Food Program, providing food for people living with HIV/AIDS. Food rations were provided through a community organization called Meeting Point. It was gratifying working to prolong the life of people who were suffering from AIDS.

In another incident, I worked with one of the government ministers to distribute grinding machines to women's groups for grinding corn and also generate. The joy on their faces was incredible. I remember going to monitor the project, and I found that the women had accumulated some savings and were now lending money to the group members.

All my life, I have wanted to serve people and make their lives better while improving their situation. That is why I have always worked in rural areas, poor communities and even in war zones. Amazed at my nature of work, one of my cousins, Dr. Godfrey Akileng, said, "Samuel is a missionary."

I believe true success is not determined by the resources a person accumulates but rather the services rendered to the vulnerable.

When a person offers to serve others, there is fulfillment. Jesus is an example. He healed, fed and assisted many people, including comforting bereaved families.

In my community, a school project was initiated by the community and we have been engaged in developing the school and giving poor kids opportunities for better education. A lot of people wonder why I participated in such projects. It is merely serving my gift. I know myself and my origin and history. I know what it means not to have shoes while going to class for examinations. I know what it means to go to bed hungry while trying to get education. I rode a bicycle for several kilometers to collect food to bring to town for use during school term. I was naturally born to serve and I am making a difference.

I am convinced that a true leader is one who knows him or herself. A true leader is not afraid of their past; instead, they have discovered who they are and have the will to serve people to improve their lives. One of the best examples of a true leader is my brother-in-law, Mr. Simon Anguria. He is a lucky person. We have worked on several projects together.

He is always the first person called when there is a problem. He has manifested his leadership potential. He is always offering himself to serve others: the in-laws, community, or school committees, etc. He is the first person called when someone is sick. When someone dies, he gets information and people look to him for solutions to their problems. I believe he found his purpose and is using his potential to fulfill that purpose.

What about you?

To me, Simon Anguria is a leader in his own right. He serves the people around his community in various ways, and he has influence. He is a transformed person and continues to transform society. In Bukedea Christian High School where he serves as Resident Advisor, he has planted trees in the school compound. When I look at the trees, I am reminded that they will live for years after we all die. The school will enable future generations to attain a quality education. He has a desire to serve, and because of that, he is always sought after in the community.

Factors that Contribute to Emergence of Leaders

Leaders emerge when any of the following conditions prevail:

1. **Pressure or tragedy:** When there is pressure; a leader will emerge.

2. **Oppression:** A leader will emerge when a community is oppressed or persecuted. All leaders such as Mandela (South Africa), Nyerere (Tanzania), Kenyatta (Kenya), Obote (Uganda), Garang (South Sudan) and others emerged because they were fighting against oppression. They fought against colonial rule, oppression and gained independence. Persecution drove them to fight against oppressors and oppression.

3. **Circumstances:** Circumstances such as poverty or poor living conditions can produce a leader. Mother Teresa was an unknown Catholic nun but she died as a leader. When she observed millions of Indian people suffering and begging in the streets, she decided to offer herself to serve those poor people.

4. **Leadership Training and Development:** In some cases, leaders emerge through training, development, and experiences.

Examples of Leaders that God Used

1. **Moses:** He led a group of slaves from oppression to the Promised Land. Moses was not charismatic. He had a problem speaking, but God gave him the ability to lead. He had a brother, Aaron, who became his public spokesman.

2. **David:** He was the youngest child in Jesse's family. God sent Samuel to anoint him as a leader to replace Saul who disobeyed God's commandments. David was a leader; he made mistakes, killed his general and married that man's wife. David defeated his enemies.

3. **Other Leaders in the Bible:** Joshua, Solomon, Esther, Stephen, Peter, and Timothy among others.

The Leadership Development and Discovery Process

Jesus was near the sea of Galilee when He saw four folks (Mark 1:14-20). He told them to *"follow Me and I will make you fishers of men."* When I studied the words "fishers of men," it means they were to go through a process. Any person who emerges as a leader without going through a process will destroy humanity. They will manipulate, oppress or even destroy the destines of people and the coming generations.

Peter and eleven disciples went through the process, which included training, coaching, testing, and sharing experiences with their leader before becoming what they were supposed to be -- "fishers of men."

Real leaders never oppress people, but serve them. They do not claim God has sent them. They merely serve the people, and people are happy with them. True leaders never get elected, but they pursue their purpose.

In Uganda, there is a musician known as Jose Chameleon who is known as Joseph Mayanja. This guy is a leader in the entertainment industry. He discovered the gift of singing and playing of music. That gift has taken him to different parts of the world. He has his education, but the gift has made him to meet different people and dignitaries. He serves his gift.

There are Four Challenges Humans Have to Face:

1. Discovering their personal gifts and serving those gifts to the world.
2. Getting to know who they are. Most people never discover who they are. They do not know themselves.
3. Finding why they exist on Earth. What is their purpose for living?
4. When they find their purpose, they must lose themselves for the sake of their purpose.

There are a lot of people who are educated but never know their gifts. They have never asked questions in the hearts of human beings. Questions like: Who am I? What can I do? Why am I on Earth? Jesus told the disciples why He came to Earth; He said I did not come to be served but to serve. He knew His reason for being on this planet. If human being gets answers to the questions I have listed in the paragraph below, they are most likely to discover their leadership in life.

1. Who am I?
2. What can I serve to the world?
3. What prototype can I offer?
4. Am I willing to be a slave to my gift?
5. Am I willing to be the youngest in a group?
6. What is my true ability?
7. What can I do that means and bring joy to my life?
8. Will it benefit the people?
9. What gifts do I possess which help others?

You cannot go to college to get answers to those questions. You can not get answers from your friends or family even though they can try to give you their ideas and views. The answers to those questions will come through self-discovery.

I remember when a colleague at the United Nations Children's Fund (UNICEF) told me I could never become an international expatriate. This person judged me because of my background, education, current position, and experience. The person had no idea about my gifts.

The same is true with you. There are individuals who have already judged you. They have told you that you cannot be a leader. You are not gifted. You come from a wrong part of the country. You are not from a royal family. You are not from the right tribe or clan. You are poor. You have no history. You lack experience.

Another person may have said that you cannot manage to lead others. You do not have leadership blessings, gifts or charisma. I believe millions of people have been told this, and now those things have affected them. They may never reach their potential.Never let this assertions get you down. Understand that those people are ignorant and do not know you. They have no idea of the limitless potential God placed inside of you. There are a lot of individuals who already know a little bit about you, but the truth is that they do not know everything about you.

The Practical Steps to Self-Discovery

Proverbs 19:21 says, *"Many are the plans in a man's heart but it is the Lord's purpose that prevails."* God's purpose is more powerful than man's plans or ideas. When you answer the following questions, you will get the steps to self-discovery:

1. What is God's purpose for me?

2. What are my inherent and deepest desires? Psalms 37:4 states that God will give you the desires of your heart.

3. What things are you willing to lose in life? Remember that Jesus said that if any man desires to follow him, the person must forget himself.

4. What gifts do you have that you can serve to your generation?

5. What things are you passionate about that you want to be doing?

6. What are ideas, thoughts that keep lingering in your mind? The things you wish to be doing?

7. What are you seeing or imagining? What vision do you have that will make a difference in the world and benefit humanity?

8. What can you offer to humanity and the next generation after you are gone?

9. What would you love to do that will bring more meaning and fulfillment to your life and others around you? Is it a job, a project, a career, or community social group training?

10. What problem is your community facing that you wish to solve? Does it make you angry or unhappy?

Is Leadership an End or a Process?

Leadership is not a right. Leadership is a process. Every leader goes through a process to eventually become a leader. Moses was a leader, grew up in a palace, went to the desert and lived there for forty years. When He returned to Egypt, he led the people to the Promised Land. Joshua was a leader. He spent forty years with Moses and the Israelites in the desert before taking on leadership role.

PREPARE
TO SERVE YOUR
LEADERSHIP GIFTS

13

Develop Your Own Philosophy

Be the change that you wish
to see in the world.
Mahatma Gandhi

Understanding the Concept of "Philosophy"

The word "philosophy" comes from two words: "philo" which means "love" and "sophy," which means to think of or know of. Our personal thoughts produce our philosophy. Philosophy simply means being in love your thoughts, ideas or wisdom. King Solomon said something in connection to thoughts. *"For as he thinks in his heart, so is he."* (Proverbs 23:7). This implies or means that the thoughts in your mind determine who you will become. Our thoughts determine the outcomes of our life and what happens in the future. When you look at the statement made by Solomon, notice the word "heart."

In the Hebrew language, the concept of heart does not mean the organ in your chest but rather the "hidden mind," or what we call the subconscious mind. When you receive information, it is stored first in the conscious mind before being transferred to the subconscious mind. When treating a person with mental problems, psychologists attempt to reconstruct the subconscious mind. When Jesus was with His disciples, He taught them about the heart. *"For out of the abundance of the heart the mouth speaks."* (Matthew 12:34)

He also mentioned this in Matthew 15:18-20:

> *But those things which proceed out of the mouth come from the heart, and they defile a man. For out of the heart proceed evil thoughts, murders, adulteries, fornications, thefts, false witness, and blasphemies. These are the things which defile a man, but to eat with unwashed hands does not defile a man.*

When I read these teachings as a teenager, I noticed that the things we say are what destroys a human being. Our words that come from our thoughts kill us. When actions are born from our hearts they are manifested in the form of deeds. Our thoughts and ideas dictate, guide and lead us into our attitudes and lives. Philosophy, as I have said, is the foundation of our leadership, and therefore, it is the most important thing that determines our personal beliefs, attitudes, and actions.

When they say to you that you will not make it, they are all lying to you. Your duty is to believe God. You can achieve anything that God gives you in your mind. You can become the leader you are meant to be. If a manufacturer made a plane to fly, it can fly if the right conditions are in place. The same is true with you and God.

Education, training, background or management training is good, but my concern is what your belief system is. What ideas do you have? What do you believe about yourself and the people around you? If you change your ideas, your life becomes different. Words are hidden thoughts in our minds.

Let me say something about education, training or learning experiences you might have received. All these things are good, but the danger is that education is based on a curriculum. A school curriculum is a system where the course content is decided by a particular group of people who, on completion of the same training, have the same characteristics or behaviors. A curriculum is a predetermined result of outcomes on the learners, and sometimes, it imposes limitations on the student's ability or capacity.

The Power of Ideas, Words and Thoughts

If there is anything I have come to appreciate in my short journey on Earth, it is the powerful force of ideas, thoughts or words. Thoughts are found in the mind, so are ideas. When spoken, thoughts become words. Words create actions and consequences. Ideas are the most powerful force in the world because everything that is visible today is the result of ideas. Ideas have created everything. The computer I used to type the book was at one time an idea.

There are many reasons people never believe in themselves. One of them is that they do not even believe in their personal philosophy. Every human being is a philosopher. A philosopher loves wisdom, and they spend time understanding truth and knowledge about certain things in life. Some people do not believe in their ideas because of their past or historical background.

If you want to change the course of destiny for your life, you must first believe in yourself. You must believe you were created by God and born to lead. People have abandoned their ideas because of doubt and fear. The ideas you think of every day are your potential, and you have the capacity to turn those ideas into things that are visible because only you know or think of those ideas. No one thinks the same way as you.

When I discuss leadership, people tend to think of Presidents, Ministers, Members of Parliament, Counsellors or politicians. Leaders are all around us. Leaders are in church, schools, hospitals and businesses. That means leaders are everywhere. I believe leadership is available everywhere and in every person.

The majority of people have been miseducated and manipulated into thinking that leadership is only for the privileged, especially those who can speak well in public. They were taught in our schools or colleges by the lecturers, teachers or professors. The majority of individuals have taken those ideas, and today I want to advise you to renew your mind and change the way you think about leaders and leadership. What ideas do you imagine? What are your personal beliefs about who you are? What is your personal life philosophy?

God's Eternal Word

John 1:1-5 says,

> In the beginning was the Word, and the Word was with God, and the Word was God. He was at the beginning with God. All things were made through Him, and without Him nothing was made that was made. In Him was life, and the life was the light of men. And the light shines in the darkness, and the darkness did not comprehend it.

I want you to replace "word" with idea or thought. Notice that words come from the thoughts that God had. The thought was God's idea. The ideas that God had created everything. All things were created by He who had the word, thought or idea. Everything in life is a result of ideas, or thoughts; this includes leadership, management, science or technology among many things.

The Thinking Process

When we think of something, ideas get formed. If we see something, our brain is activated. We begin to analyze, interpret and internalize it. When we finally accept the ideas, an internal transfer takes place and ideas go from the conscious mind to subconscious mind. I want to call this a "fixed deposit account." The ideas that accumulate in the fixed deposit account becomes the belief system, and thus our philosophy about life. Those ideas in the fixed deposit account we retrieve, apply, use, and live because we consider them to be true, correct or right. They say experience is the best teacher. I do not agree with this. Experience is the best teacher if it does not rely on tradition.

Every person lives and makes decisions based on their beliefs. The most dangerous thing I have come to note in life is that people will try to make you what they want you to be. Do not take ideas from people carelessly, but instead seek for the truth. If you are told something long enough, you will begin to believe it. Those ideas get stored in the fixed deposit account that I talked about that is the subconscious mind.

The other beautiful and unusual side of idea transfer is that it can benefit society. If parents transfer to their kids the importance of respect to elders, society will have people who respect each other. If children are taught discipline, this will also be manifested in

179

responsible leaders. Values and traditions are transferred to younger generations through teaching, oral histories, and training. In societies where conflicts have been the order of the day, kids never think of peace instead they practice violence or conflict.

What Do You Believe About You?

The majority of people often ask, "What do others think about me?" But to me the most important thing is what will Jesus say on the final Day of Judgment. That moment is when Jesus, with the assistance of the angels, separates the sheep from goats. When we absorb and internally accept what our families, friends or peers think, we tend to believe what they think to be true, and we accept that.

If you keep hearing something over a period and often, you will begin to believe it as the truth. I recall in my country, a lot of things have been told about our first generation of leaders. Over time, I started to believe them because the story was told by one side while the other side never had a chance to respond. As soon as you believe what is said to you, you will begin to respond based on the belief system that has been established for you. If you are constantly told you will not succeed, you will believe it.

To change your belief systems, you need God's Spirit in your life; you also need mentors or coaches to help you develop your gifts, talents, potential and knowledge. It will help you improve your self-image and awareness about you and change the thoughts pattern in your life. In fact, the Bible says do not accept or believe the opinion, views or words other people say about you. Paul wrote it down, and I will never forget it: *"Let God be true but every man a liar."* (Romans 3:4).

The Power of Systems

Reflect on the Labor Party or Conservative Party Systems in Britain. Think about Democrats and the Republicans in the USA. Reflect on the parties in Germany. Think about the African National Congress (ANC). Think about National Resistance Movement (NRM) in Uganda. Think about parties in Israel. Now think about the education systems. Think about the health systems. Think about government systems. Think of financial systems. All of these are systems. What is happening in the world today is a result of systems. In a system, there is a way things are supposed to be done. You cannot change the system from outside. You must do it from within.

Education Systems are Responsible for job Seekers

The education systems have created job seekers, not job creators. We have been trained to work for money, not the other way around. Our parents or teachers have been responsible for making their kids followers instead of leaders. Can you imagine if you start telling your child from age five that they are leaders and what that will means by age 20? He or she will behave, act and become a leader.

There are millions of people whose ability or potential has been destroyed by systems. They never discovered who they were. I recall meeting a lady in Nigeria who was afraid of her culture and what people would say about her. I told her, the words "culture" and "religion" are two things that I consider dangerous and must be studied before application. Ideas and teachings from any culture or religion must be examined carefully about the truth it conveys to people. It is better to believe in God who does not lie. Today, that lady's confidence and self-esteem have been repaired. There are millions of people who are like her, but their conditions of life are still the same. You need to change your belief system. Become different.

Jesus' Leadership Model

If you study the life of Jesus, you will notice some things. First, this man was born in a place called Bethlehem, in a manger. He lived with his parents in a village called Nazareth. The Roman system dominated the area. He was considered a non-citizen. All the forces that could hold a person down were present. He went to the Sea of Galilee one time and met a group of fishermen. He told them to come and be part of his team with the assurance of making them "fishers of men." I want you to imagine the fishermen. What kind of people were these men? I believe they were the least in the society.

The disciples became global leaders. How did Jesus do that? He never went to the best school, college or university. Yet, He will remain the world's most influential leader, and if you believe that, decide to follow his model. He never followed the culture of his day but instead followed God's ideas or words.

All that Jesus said was that He was the Son of God. In other words, He was saying, "I am a human being just like you, but I have used what I was born with to become and emerge as a leader." Jesus was able to overcome all his childhood limitations and transformed a group of people to lead a local organization into a global one. Matthew 11:19 says, *"The Son of Man came eating and drinking, and they say, 'Look, a glutton and a winebibber, a friend of tax collectors and sinners!' But wisdom is justified by her children."*

Jesus Christ understood that all human beings were created to lead and each leads based on the gift they possess. It is hard to believe such ideas because of the historical problems associated with our past experiences. The area where you succeed is where you gift lies. If you want to lead, you need to follow other leaders who will teach you how to lead. Jesus started to alter the thinking of the fishermen by telling them he will make them "fishers of men." In other words, He told them His philosophy.

What Happens When Ideas Change?

If you change your ideas, you will begin to think differently and your actions will manifest this change. People will start to believe you are going against their expectations. All that you have become today is a result of the ideas you have believed. If you are not successful or leading in some area, it's because of your belief system. Jesus being born in the lowest part of Israel came to confirm that God created people as leaders. That is why he chose the least, not the greatest. Some people think you will never amount to anything. Do not accept those ideas. Seek knowledge about who you are and start to serve others. If you discover your gift and develop a positive attitude, your leadership potential will appear and you will influence your generation.

Develop a Can-Do Attitude

Attitude towards life can be changed by circumstances, problems, setbacks or opportunities. The way you react to life is directly proportional to your attitude. You have a gift that nobody else has. The discovery of yourself is what will change your attitude and altitude.

During my own journey, I used to blame others for my situation. I used to think if my mother was alive, I would be better than I am now. My attitude was negative. I had self-doubt as a kid, but when I began to believe in myself, my life changed and improved. Attitude determines the confidence in a person. Self-confidence comes from the knowledge of self.

Some people have been taught how to think positively, and they still have negative attitudes. Education does not give you attitude; beliefs do. Your leadership will only be born the day you decide to start serving others, reject the opinion of others, and pursue your dreams.

Let's refresh our thinking. There was a group of twelve Israelites that were chosen and sent to spy out the Promised Land when they crossed River Jordan after spending forty years in the wilderness. The assignment was given by Moses. When they brought back the report to him, ten of them said that they seemed like grasshoppers in the eyes of the inhabitants while two were emphatic that they should go in and take up their land. Here are two different groups. One reacts negatively and other positively.

I believe that the only way people can discover who they are is through a change in attitudes and thinking. Without a change in the information stored in your mind, or "brain bank," nothing can change. People behave the way they are because of the information they have received or have been receiving. The attitude must change from being negative to having fruits of the Spirit. Apostle Paul wrote a letter to believers in the early Christian community in Galatia:

But the fruit of the Spirit is love, joy, peace, longsuffering, kindness, goodness, faithfulness, gentlenesses, and self-control. Against such, there is no law. And those who are Christ's have crucified the flesh with its passions and desires. If we live in the Spirit, let us also walk in the Spirit. Let us not become conceited, provoking one another, envying one another. (Galatians 5:22-26)

Perception Affects Results, Outcomes and Decisions

Then Caleb quieted the people before Moses, and said, "Let us go up at once and take possession, for we are well able to overcome it." But the men who had gone up with him said, "We are not able to go up against the people, for they are stronger than we." And they gave the children of Israel a bad report of the land which they had spied out, saying, "The land through which we have gone as spies is a land that devours its inhabitants, and all the people whom we saw in it are men of great stature. There we saw the giants (the descendants of Anak came from the giants), and we were like grasshoppers in our sight, and so we were in their sight. (Numbers 13:31-33)

Why do People Have Negative Attitude?

There are many possible reasons:

1. **Fear that is generated by self:** God promised this land to the people of Israel. They witnessed miracles. They drank free water in the desert and were given manna from heaven

185

but they still had a negative attitude and self-doubt. They were destined to reach their destination but never believed in themselves and God.

2. **Oppression and negative reinforcement:** When these two are combined with self-hatred, devaluation, a sense of unworthiness and lack of self-confidence, the results will be a negative attitude.

3. **Lack or poor self- esteem and self-destructive behaviors:** The lack of self-esteem negatively impacts the ability of people to achieve their destiny. The teaching from schools and colleges and associations have made people believe they cannot change their personal circumstances and improve their lives.

When I was growing up during university days, I watched a couple of friends who went to bars and spent all their money buying alcohol. They told me that part of Teso culture requires them to drink. When I watched what happened after drinking, I said my culture is bad and I will not be part of that group. As I speak today, some of those people have died. Guess what killed them? Culture, influence from bad friends and wrong belief systems.

Those young men were potential leaders, but their destiny was shortlived. Their leadership was destroyed by groups, bad influence, confusion, and disillusionment. I believe if they had different beliefs the story would be different. I am talking about computer scientists, agricultural engineers, and surveyors. It is my belief that instead of drinking and if they used those skills in productive areas, society would be a different place today.

Jesus Asked the Disciples, "Who Do You Say I Am?"

As Jesus taught his disciples about kingdom life here on Earth, one day He asked them, "Who do people say I am?" They answered Him by saying, "You are the Christ" (Matthew 16:13-17). People often associate you with your past, background or environment, but they do not know you. Nobody knows you except God. Your family or friends know a little about you but not everything.

The greatest problem that people continue to face in life is self-doubt. There are millions of people who question themselves. You might have been called all sorts of words stupid, lazy, idiotic, inadequate and so on. Never believe these words because if you do, they become your belief system. When Jesus came to the world, He came and restored our confidence and killed our self-doubt. He did things to disapprove those who said He was nothing more than a carpenter's son. The Bible says God became flesh and lived among us so that we could see His true glory. If we believe in Jesus' words, we will become leaders.

Jesus told the fishermen at the Sea of Galilee "Follow Him;" they agreed and followed Him. Do you know the end of the story? Peter became a great leader. Paul traveled from one territory spreading the Good News of the kingdom. He spent his life speaking to others about leadership, dominion, transformation, and rulership. My question to you is: Are you willing to follow someone who has called you? Are you willing to be mentored? Are you ready to submit to that person? If so, then you are on your way to the top spot in life.

It must be noted that true leaders always change things and situations. For example, Jesus Christ, whom I consider the greatest leader in time and off-time did great things and changed circumstances. He did things that are unimaginable from such a humble background. He walked on water. He spoke to the tree to die, and the tree died. He talked to the fishermen who laboured all night without catching anything. Afterwards, they threw their nets into the sea and they caught massive number of fishes as a result of their obedience to Jesus' commandments. Jesus stopped the storm that was going to cause the disciples to drown. He even multiplied the fish and loaves of bread (John 6:1-14)

The Principles and Takeaways

1. Leaders must have compassion over their followers.
2. Leaders work with the people who follow them.
3. Leaders assess the needs of people and meet those needs.
4. Leaders use the available resources to meet the needs or solve their problems.
5. Leaders never waste resources instead they manage the resources effectively.

True Leaders Give Authority to Followers

Jesus was never afraid of His followers. He gave them the authority He had received from God, His Father from Heaven. How many leaders do we have today who are afraid of giving up power? Are those real leaders? We need to learn from the example of Jesus Christ in Luke 9:1-6.

Jesus knew He was both the Son of Man and the Son of God. We have in our world today leaders who are afraid of their followers taking power and authority away from them. But Jesus gave His disciples power. It is amazing when the disciples returned and gave testimonies of their work and field experience. They testified that they were able to change the situation or improve the lives of others. If you are a leader in any setting today, are you willing to give up power and authority?

True Leaders Give Power to Followers

True leaders like Jesus were never afraid of the success of others or their followers. I recall reading a story about a national leader who went with his minister to one of the countries in the west. When the minister did well in a meeting, the national leader was not impressed. Upon their return from a foreign trip, the minister was found dead in his home town. What happened? What a tragedy and what a type of leaders we have in our world! Leadership is not about eliminating those who achieve results, instead it is the ability to inspire others through influence to achieve common goals.

The Fig Tree Withered

Now in the morning, as He returned to the city, He was hungry. And seeing a fig tree by the road, He came to it and found nothing on it but leaves, and said to it, *"Let no fruit grow on you ever again."* Immediately the fig tree withered away. (Matthew 21:18-19)

The principle behind the fig tree is that some people will be cut off before they manifest their fruits. Are you going be like the fig tree in your generation?

The Relationship Between Faith and Doubt

Faith and doubt are not friends but enemies. The two cannot co-exist at the same time. Faith must overcome doubt. Jesus said that He spoke to the tree and saw what happened to the tree. He told the disciples that they could tell the mountain to move if they have the faith and it must be done without doubt. God is depressed when we have doubt. God is pleased when we have faith (Hebrews 11:6). When you have faith, God rewards you and when you have doubt, He ignores your prayers. The key here is faith, and with belief, it is possible to move mountains. Some people have problems as big as mountains, and they are confused on what to do. You need faith to move on past the problems. You need to get past your fears into your faith in God. It is important to note that there is nothing as dangerous as doubt. Doubt comes from unbelief and a lack of self-esteem. Doubt is the enemy of success and progress.

What Quantity of Faith do we Need?

When you study the Holy Scripture, you will find instances where Jesus says one needs the smallest amount of faith to move mountains. Matthew 17: 20 says:

> So Jesus said to them, "Because of your unbelief; for assuredly, I say to you, if you have faith as a mustard seed, you will say to this mountain, 'Move from here to there,' and it will move, and nothing will be impossible for you. However, this kind does not go out except by prayer and fasting.

The size of a mustard seed is the faith that God expects you as a believer to have. Faith makes things that seem impossible become possible.

Affirmations to Change Negative Thoughts

After many years of wrong teaching, false beliefs and conditioned responses to life, it is not easy to convince yourself that you are born to lead. If you are going to change your beliefs, you need to start reminding yourself that you have the ability to lead. Psychologists and sociologists have concluded that if you keep affirming to yourself some positive statements even what is impossible will be eventually accomplished.

Here are some of the most powerful affirmations that you might need to read and speak to yourself over and over again within a six-month period:

- I know my purpose and reason for living on Earth.
- I have a vision for my life that I will share with others.
- I love serving others and am passionate about serving others.
- I have unlimited potential inside of me, but I must understand it.
- I have already set my goals and I am going to pursue those goals.
- I will develop my faith in God to have spiritual strength to overcome crisis.
- I have the capacity to learn and teach others. I will study and read to gain more knowledge.
- I am constantly improving my knowledge and skills.
- I believe God created all people and I value them all.
- I will be confident and bold in actions that lead to my vision.
- I am a person of integrity and I will keep my integrity intact.
- I will take advantage of all good opportunities and use my time to achieve the goals I have set to accomplish.

- I am a leader and I was born to rule, dominate and lead by God.
- I am self-motivated, responsible and accountable.

Know The Leadership Toolbox

To become a leader,
you must become a follower first.
Dr. Samuel Odeke, DSL

Effective Preparation is Critical for Leadership

Even though you have the abilities and knowledge to carry out some tasks, you still need to prepare adequately. The Lord Jesus Christ said something that still puzzles me in Matthew 20:26: "Whoever wants to be great." Before you engage in any significant endeavor, you must prepare so that it will succeed.

What features do effective leaders have in common in your community? You will notice they have some things that make them ready or prepared to lead. Some have an education. Some have experience. Some have knowledge. Some have skills.

When you look at the tools inside their toolbox, you might see that they inspire people. Inspiring means that you make people interested in your vision, ideas, plans, goals, and values.

True leaders have the capacity to inspire people and they never manipulate those who follow them. Instead they are inspired by their vision and purpose and passion. Real leaders lead by example so that others can follow them. The opposite is also true: leaders who manipulate others threaten, frighten and make unrealistic promises.

The True Source of Inspiration, Passion and Motivation

Inspiration is related to the breath of God. To inspire means to inhale, which is a Latin word that implies to "breathe in". God breathed into humans the capacity to be fruitful, multiply and dominate. In other words, God inspired people to lead. Leadership is simply having the capability of influencing others by inspiring them. In this definition, we see key terms that form the foundation of leadership.

The Following Words are Key:

1. **Capacity:** Ability, power, potential or energy. A leader cannot lead without capacity. There must be some gifts, skills, and knowledge.

2. **Influence:** Dominating and working with others. It is not the same as manipulation.

3. **Inspiration:** To breathe life, give life or energy or inhale energy. Some leaders do not inspire their followers but manipulate or threaten them. The same is with some parents; they harass as well as intimidate their kids. If you want to inspire your children to do great things, you will have to

show them how that happens. In Uganda, Janet Museveni, Winfred Byanyima, and Miria Matembe are examples of leaders who inspire others, particularly the young women.

4. **Passion:** It is the greatest desire to do something. Passion can also be a source of inspiration. If you have a passion for doing something, then you can inspire them and end up influencing them.

5. **Vision:** A preferred future or purpose. Every correct vision usually has one believer at first. If you study vision in Scripture, you will see that every true vision from God always has one believer fast. Moses was given a vision for delivering the Israelites to the Promised Land. Joseph saw a vision in a dream about his family. Leaders are produced by the vision, and it is the vision that separates a leader from followers. As leaders dare and decide to pursue their leadership, the vision will be tested by obstacles, setbacks, problems or rejection by those who might benefit from the vision. When such things happens, you need to believe in your vision. Continue with your plans because only God knows the purpose for giving a vision to a leader.

6. **Conviction:** Your convictions must be so compelling to the point of making you a slave, and you are willing to pay any price even if it costs your life, friends and all the valuable things that you cherish. Nelson Mandela was locked in prison for 27 years but had a conviction that apartheid was evil and dangerous. He achieved his vision of freedom from apartheid.

7. **Purpose:** This is the original reason for the creation of a product or thing. Products are manufactured to meet a need. For instance, a car is made to solve transportation problems. No manufacturer makes a product without knowing its purpose. The same is true about you and me. We have a purpose on Earth. God created us to accomplish something. There is something that God desired that made Him create or manufacture us.

How Does one Become a Leader?

If you discover a problem in your community that needs to be solved and you think it is the biggest problem, then you have found a purpose. To become a leader, you need to have a passion for something. Vision generates passion that is born out of a conviction in the heart of a leader, and that belief produces a sense of significance I call purpose. The purpose is the reason you exist. To discover purpose, you must ask the creator or manufacturer. The user of the product might know the purpose, but the manufacturer knows the purpose in the details.

God knows the purpose He created you . For a leader to emerge, they must have all seven elements listed above. When a leader discovers their purpose and sees the vision (preferred future, destiny), leadership and influence is the result. If someone claims or wants to be a leader without the will to pursue their vision, followers will not be attracted to the leader. Leadership is born when people decide to pursue their vision, believe in their convictions and stand by their principles and values and protect their character.

How Does a Product Accomplish its Purpose?

Let us consider a vehicle that has to take people from one location to another approximately 1,000 km away. The car will achieve that purpose by persisting and persevering. The same applies to your original purpose. You have to be persistent and persevere that must be combined with passion and conviction as you view the vision as destiny. True leaders do not seek leadership: they pursue their original assignment with purpose. They do not pursue followers but inspire followers about their purpose and with passion and conviction.

The real origin of leadership is a vision fueled by passion and conviction. That is why leaders are willing to pursue their purpose at the cost of their personal lives. True leaders have the willingness to pursue their purpose because they believe what they are doing is worth dying for.

Everything Has a Purpose

Every manufacturer creates or manufactures products for a reason. If you have a desire to know why a product exists, ask the manufacturer. Ask God to reveal the purpose for your existence. You can read God's book to establish a relationship with God, and without a relationship with God, you will never accomplish your purpose. Proverbs 19: 21 says, *"Many are the plans in a man's heart, but it is the Lord's purpose that will prevail."*

It teaches the following fundamental truths:

1. God is always motivated by a sense of purpose.
2. God creates and does everything for a purpose.

197

3. God's purpose is important than man's plans.
4. God's purpose is better man's plans.
5. God's purpose will prevail over man's purpose.
6. Consult God for your purpose and proceed to make your plans.
7. Pursuing God's purpose is a key to success.

Have you seen people who started things and ended up abandoning them? It is because God's purpose is bigger than man's plans and ideas. You might go to college to get a degree but end up abandoning the course and career. It means they did not consult God before starting a college degree and they devise their plans without involving God. It is after they have failed in their plans that people backtrack and run back to God. The key to fulfilment in life is to always enquire from God before starting anything or make plans. Ask God approve the plans by putting his name on them.

Every human being with a plan must dedicate their plans to God for them to succeed. God is the one Who determines the purpose because He is the manufacturer, the Creator. Ideally, God creates out of nothing. The most important thing about knowing and discovering your purpose is to naturally become free from your past. You become like Jesus Christ Who said, *"Now my soul is troubled, and what shall I say? 'Father, save me from this hour'? No, it was for this very reason I came to this hour."* (John 12:27)

When you understand your reason for existence, you will walk against all obstacles and setbacks; you will withstand attacks and criticism because you have seen a vision. No matter who tries to put you down, intimidate or attack you while pursuing the plans God has approved, you will overcome because you are convinced about your vision. You become unstoppable because you are passionate about what you are doing.

Who are True Leaders?

Leaders are people who have discovered their purpose and decided that no matter what happens, they will continue with the struggle. Leaders decide that they have to solve a problem by offering their gifts. They have the commitment to do all it takes to bring change and make society a better place through the serving of their gifts.

When you believe in your purpose and you are convicted about it, keep pressing on. Those who oppose you will come and join you as you fulfill your calling. Joseph was thrown into a pit by his brothers because of his dreams. He was sold to traders by his brothers. They told his father that he was dead. In Egypt, the rulers put Joseph in jail, but he endured all this pain. In the end, Pharaoh made him a leader. This position made Jospeh a planner and disaster specialist when famine hit Egypt. Later, when his family was afflicted by famine they went to Egypt and met the same man they attacked, but Joseph forgave them and saved his family lineage. Sometimes the people who are closest to you will turn against you. Do not worry but remind yourself you are going through these tests but will emerge and win.

Also, leaders who have developed a conviction for what they believe do not even have time to go on vacation as they want, to finish what they started. Jesus Christ used the statement that is common to real leaders by saying, *"It is finished"* (John 19:30). Another true leader, Paul, said something at the end of his assignment: *"I have fought the good fight, I have finished the race, I have kept the faith"* (2 Timothy 4:7).

See the similarity of attitudes. Both said the word "finished." I believe the greatest statement a leader can make is, "I have finished." When you finish your purpose then you can move to the next level for a reward from your Heavenly Father, our God. God is interested in finishers rather than professional beginners. Millions of people begin or start things but never finish. They quit when the going gets rough.

We have examples of leaders who influenced millions of people but ended up in a horrible way: Adolf Hitler, Saddam Hussein, and Muammar Gaddafi. They influenced people by manipulation and intimidation. Real leaders inspire and empower people.

The Mindset of True Leaders

As leaders discover what they are supposed to do, they might behave in strange ways. They may start to believe so much in their ideas and hold the belief that everyone around them is a joker. A leader suddenly gets confidence and does not care about their past mistakes and behaviors. All they are concerned with is their vision. Sometimes people who have no purpose are the ones who are interested in parties or having holidays. But individuals with a purpose do not have time for leisure. They hate sleep; they work hard and hate poverty. They have no time to rest. Look at what King Solomon said; *"Do not love sleep or you will grow poor; stay awake, and you will have food to spare"* (Proverbs 20:13). Whenever a leader discovers their purpose cum passion, they begin to hate the things that distract them from their original intent.

A Leader's Toolbox

Leadership is not a simple matter. A leader needs the following in his or her leadership box:

1. **Faith:** A leader must be full of faith and faithfulness

2. **Potential:** A leader must manifest the leadership capacity

3. **Proven integrity:** A leader should have integrity

4. **Trustworthiness:** A leader must be trustworthy.

5. **Sense of responsibility:** A leader must have responsibility and finish the job before quitting.

6. **Positive self-image:** A leader should know their self, value and worth and be active all the time.

7. **Knowledge and skills and competence:** A leader must be knowledgeable. He must be a learner and reader and must not graduate from the school of learning.

8. **Servant attitude:** A leader must submit and listen to advice of those he leads.

9. **Self-discipline:** A leader must set standards for the greater vision and purpose. Leaders set standards for excellence. There must be self-control and obedience to laws.

10. **Ideas:** Have original ideas and be able to train others. Seek new ideas and knowledge. Have a capacity to think.

11. **Concepts:** Develop your personal ideas about what you believe is right with God's word.

12. **Humility:** A leader must be stable and humble but not arrogant.

13. **Flexibility:** A leader must be flexible and does not refuse to change but be ready to adapt and make adjustments.

14. **Planning ability:** Must have the capacity to set goals and targets.

15. **Experience:** Must have served and acquired experience for leading others and have a sense of maturity.

16. **Resilience:** A leader must be able to withstand pressure, attacks and challenges and bounce back after an attack or fall.

17. **Sense of humor:** A leader must have moments when they can laugh at the life they live without being serious all the time. They should laugh at themselves, have a fun time and laugh even during times of crisis.

18. **Friendliness:** A leader must have interpersonal skills so that people are comfortable with him or her. A leader cannot be a friend to all people but should have a friendly attitude.

19. **Morals:** A leader must have morals and manage their household problems. Must manage family to avoid taking those issues to work.

20. **Character and ethics:** A leader must have a character that is stable as a statue and behave ethically at all times.

21. **Learning:** A leader does not stop learning but continues to learn to grow their leadership, to get knowledge, have information and understanding. Leaders never graduate from the "school of learning."

22. **Courage:** A leader must have the will to take on risks. Also have the will to stand alone when everyone is silent or in opposition, including making hard decisions.

The Benefits of Servant Leadership

The following are the benefits of servant leadership:

- Servant leaders give a leader authority to lead. Authority is the ability to execute your roles and responsibilities. Jesus taught the disciples after His resurrection that He has authority. Mathew 28:18-20 says,

  All authority in heaven and on Earth has been given to me. Therefore go and make disciples of all nations and teaching them to obey everything I have commanded you. And surely I am with you always, to the very end of the age.

- Servant leadership makes the leader authentic as a result of service. If you are doings things that you are not wired to do, you will find it difficult to maintain it.

- Servant leadership gives the leader a natural confidence. It means the leader will have knowledgeand the potential required to carry out the roles of leadership.

- Servant leadership gives leaders personal fulfillment. True servant leaders serve their gifts that give them personal fulfillment and pleasure of accomplishment.

- Servant leadership allows leaders to discover their intrinsic value and self-worth. The servant leader understands their personal value to the world.

- Servant leaders are interested in service not competition. They find pleasure in the success and accomplishment of others as they contribute to service of their gifts.

- Servant leadership does not compare themselves with others. Their personal value and significance do not give them security but safety. They know that every person has a gift that the leader is serving to the world.

- Servant leadership destroys jealousy because leaders know they are unique and distinctive. Servant leaders understand their purpose is a gift that nobody can take away and a unique contribution based on the intrinsic value.

- Servant leadership eliminates fear because they know what their purpose and gifts are.

- Servant leaders are calm, confident and secure. Insecurity causes fear. Low self-esteem or self-worth creates fear. Fear is a result of lack of personal vision, dream, purpose, and goals.

- Servant leaders are internally motivatedby their actions which comes from their potential, passion and purpose. They know their gifts and have an awareness of their purpose.

- Servant leaders never seek for motivation from outside motivators. They have passion that gives them energy.

15

Develop, Invest And Refine Your Gifts

A man's gift makes room
for him, and brings him
before great men.
Proverbs 18:6

The Athletes who Never Developed Their "Gifts."

When I was at Akuoro Primary School, there was a family near my home village. I believe were all gifted with a natural gift and talent to be athletes. I recall running with them during the mandatory sports events determined by the Ministry of Education. At the beginning of every first term, there would be important athletic competitions for all schools and athletes would be selected to participate at sub-county, district, regional and national levels. The athletes that excelled would qualify to participate in the next level.

As a primary school pupil, I never liked sports or athletics because I was not good at them. If we are assigned to compete I would never win. Most all the kids from that family were natural athletes, including the elder ones of whom I never attended the school. I recall listening to a story where one of the elder boys ran from Mbale to Bukedea when war broke out. I was told he ran back home within a very short period.

Similarly, I remember as kids we would always run home with the children from that family after school in the evening. It was during those early years that I discovered I was good academically and started to maximize or ensure nobody won against me during an exam. But those kids who were "natural athletes" were not good academically. The saddest thing that happened is that most of them dropped out of school and never developed their natural gifts.

There were also twin boys who happened to study with me in Kolir Primary School in Bukedea. The twins were naturally talented as good footballers. These two twins were excellent, and I still believe in my heart that they would have been great sportsmen. Each time there was a competition, the twins were playing football, and if they were selected to be on the same side, their side would win. I do not know what happened to those twins and I have not seen them in thirty years. I was told by friends that they joined the armed forces.

In both stories, the athletes were good at running marathon races and playing football. They were their natural gifts given to them by their Creator. Nobody gave the athletes these gifts. They were born with their gifts but unfortunately they never worked hard to develop and refine them. Their leadership position would have been in the area of their gifts.

As for the athletic guys who were with me in Akuoro Primary School, each time I travel back to my home village, I always meet them, but their lives are completely disoriented and wasted. The gifts are buried and potentially destroyed. When I meet them and chat, I often tell them that they used to be great runners, better than me, and we laugh it off. But as I drive away, my mind goes back to thinking about the gifts. If they had only invested in their gifts, their lives would have been much different.

One of my younger sisters is called Elizabeth (we call her Betty). This sister never had an opportunity to study or complete secondary school education because of the painful childhood experience of losing our mom. She married earlier than all of us, but one interesting thing about Betty was that she was born with a gift of selling and buying things. She does not regret having been the only one without a degree. She is happy because she does her businesses and operates her shop in a trading center in Kolir in Bukedea District. When I visit her shop, I am amazed at the way she does her business and how many people are attracted to her because of what she offers to them. On a market day, she will be transacting business and earning a living. On non-market days, she is doing her work or business in the shop, and you will find various clients coming to her to seek advice, counsel, and encouragement. She is serving her gift.

A Gift is More Important Than Education

I know this is something you might not agree with me, but it is true. Everybody was created by God with a gift just as the athletes or footballers or my sister Betty. The writer of Proverbs says these words in Proverbs 18:6: *"A man's gift makes room for him and brings him before great men."* It does not matter how educated a person becomes; if the individual does not know their gifts, they will never be a leader. That is why you find a highly educated person with a low self-esteem, timid and doing things such as sweeping toilets in some countries. You will see footballers being appointed

United Nations ambassadors because they serve their gift to the world and people pay to watch them play or entertain crowds. It is the knowledge of their gift, their uniqueness that makes them stand out and dominate the area.

The point is that each human on the planet is born with a gift. When a gift is identified, developed and invested in, it makes the person valuable and unique.

Have you read the story of Lionel Messi? Born and raised in central Argentina, Messi was diagnosed with a growth hormone deficiency as a child. At age 13, he relocated to Spain to join Barcelona, who agreed to pay for his medical treatment. After a fast progression through Barcelona's youth academy, Messi made his competitive debut aged 17 in October 2004. Despite being injury-prone during his early career, he established himself as an integral player for the club within the next three years, finishing 2007 as a finalist for both the Ballon d'Or and FIFA World Player of the Year award, a feat he repeated the following year. His first uninterrupted campaign came in the 2008–09 season, during which he helped Barcelona achieve the first treble in Spanish football. At 22 years old, Messi won the Ballon d'Or and FIFA World Player of the Year award by record voting margins.

Three successful seasons followed, with Messi winning three consecutive FIFA Ballons d'Or, including an unprecedented fourth. His personal best campaign to date was the 2011–12 season, in which he set the La Liga and European records for most goals scored in a single season, while establishing himself as Barcelona's all-time top scorer in official competitions in March 2012.

It is the gift that Messi was born with that makes him valuable and has made room for him. History cannot forget Messi. He will remain a great footballer in history. It is his gift, not the education. I know many people who are educated and not making it in life. They have all the education, and you find a business man or woman who is not educated but successful.

The Process of Becoming Valuable in Your Society

To become valuable, you must pass through a process over an extended period. Sometimes you have to go through high temperatures or pressure of life and going through various changes until you get transformed. For instance, if you want to get oil from its deposits, it takes a process of refining the crude oil to produce a valuable product. The same process occurs for gold or diamonds. Diamonds pass through high temperatures and refinement to become valuable after extraction. In the same way, every person must seek to improve their gift so that they become valuable and start the process of serving it to the community. They must work hard on themselves until they become better. There must be constant effort to learn and personally develop yourself. Personal development is the critical action to acquire knowledge, skills, competencies, self-discipline and opportunities. Personal development is therefore, crucial for value addition.

When crude oil is refined, it means impurities are removed. People who want to impact their generation or leaders need to learn this concept. They need to refine their gifts and get rid of impurities or imperfections in their lives. Impurities could be bad temper, indiscipline, abnormal behaviour, laziness, lack of values or moral character among many aspects.

The Power of Self-Worth and Self-Value

Every human being is valuable and important in their generation. They might not be rich, but they are still valuable. I recall my grandmother had leprosy. She got treated and was okay at the time we were growing as kids. My grandmother was a person of value. She had given birth to a beautiful daughter who was my mother, Joyce. Some humans see themselves as having no value. For instance, a prostitute who goes to red light districts sometimes sees themselves as valueless or children born out of wedlock.

In our societies, a lot of people have been "written off" or counted of as having no value. Our cultures have destroyed many people's lives and taught us that we have no value. It is important to know that everybody is precious and valuable. If you interact with family, friends or associates, and you find they treat you as if you have no value, you should avoid those people and associate with those persons who value as a human being.

The sense of self-worth or self-value comes from truth, self-awareness, knowledge and personal experiences that lead to self-discovery about their origin in God as a Creator. Further, leadership behavior and attitude comes forth when a person discovers their gift and serves it according to their true self without fear of comments from other people.

When a person recognizes their real value, then the views or opinion of others will no longer affect you. If you allow people's opinion to change you, you will be in bondage, and it will immobilize you from pursuing your purpose. We must get delivered from the opinions of other people that negatively affect our lives. Freedom comes from knowing the truth. Jesus Christ said, "And you shall know the truth, and the truth shall make you free." (John 8: 32)

It is not education or your government that sets you free; it is the knowledge of the truth that will make you free. Some people have no confidence because they do not know the truth about themselves. I was like this. Some people because of failure or past mistakes have given up and stopped believing in themselves.

Never Seek Approval From Others

The saddest thing I have seen in life is to seek acceptance and love from everybody. Not everyone will like or love you. I was once a people-pleaser. I was always looking for ways to please everybody. I decided to cut off my friendships with those people and we remain "Hi friends." I was becoming a victim of approval from others and pleasing others until I discovered my self-worth. Do you seek acceptance and approval from people? If so, you are in danger and about to face a crises. You might need to study on how to overcome crises. My book on Overcoming Crises is a good resource.

An individual who aspires to take on leadership roles has a sense of responsibility and obligation to make their communities, societies or nations a better one. A person becomes free if the opinion of others does not matter. An individual who is free is one who can help those who are not free or trapped by bondage. It is only God who knows you because He created you. Nobody else knows how you are made or what stuff or gifts are inside you. Only God knows that. Therefore, you must return to God your Creator to discover yourself and know why He created you.

Jesus Christ Knew Himself

When you study Scripture, you will find some important concepts about who Jesus was and why He came. In John 6, Jesus talks about Him being the Bread of Heaven or Bread of Life. Matthew 20:28 says, *"Just as the Son of Man did not come to be served, but to serve, and to give His life a ransom for many."* He said His mission was to serve not to be served. He came to give up His personal life to save many people as a ransom.

Today we are concerned with the personal protection and preservation. We want to be leaders but are unwilling to give up our lives. We wanted to be leaders but we are concerned with our personal protection.

The Qualities of True Leaders

There are no attitudes or qualities that are more important than what Paul told to the Galatian believers. He said true leaders:

- Have love for themselves and others who they lead.
- Have joy in serving and servant leadership.
- Are peacemakers, not war mongers.
- Have vision and purpose for life.
- Are able to endure long suffering.
- Must be blessed with a spirit of kindness, goodness, and faithfulness.
- Must be gentle.
- Must have self-control and personal discipline.

The Power of Value Addition Brings Success and Wealth

Everywhere I have gone in the world, I have observed that people want to be successful or achieve success in their lives, organizations or nations. I have come to a simple conclusion that people are the same even though they have different color pigmentations; they all have the same needs, problems, desires, interests and motives. Even in my little village, farmers want to succeed in their work.

If a person has a gift and they refine it, they will naturally have something of value. Success is the total of gift refinement and value addition.

I recall when a friend of mine was hired as an officer. The person was not paid highly by the employer, but the personnel officer decided to return to college for further studies. Upon completion, the personnel officer suddenly got an increase in their personal earnings, and their net worth went from one level to another.

The reason for the wage increase is because they decided to refine their gifts of handling personnel matters that resulted in an increase of their personal value and eventual success. If you look around your community, why are doctors paid highly? It is because there are very few doctors. They are rare, scarce and valuable. When a person becomes unique and valuable, they end up becoming leaders in their generation.

How Does a Person Emerge as a Leader?

The key to success and top performance in life comes from increasing value. A person can seek to get a personal coach who will help to grow his leadership capacity. A coach is a person or an individual whose task or job is to teach another person to improve his or her skills, gain more knowledge in an area like sports, music or any given field. When a coach supports you, your capacity to lead will increase, and you will be able to perform leadership roles and processes related to it. A coach will help you identify your blind spots and help you grow those areas and make you better.

Furthermore, you can also get mentored. A mentor is a wise person with a lot of knowledge and experience in an area who helps the mentee to improve. Jesus Christ was a mentor to the disciples. That is why we see Peter and other disciples emerge after Jesus Christ departed to heaven as leaders of the early church. History has leaders who emerged out of a crisis, such as post-independence leaders. They refer to themselves as "freedom fighters." But we must watch and be careful because these "freedom" fighters might be manipulators such as Hitler. Be careful to watch those who lead you. Look at Moses; he passed over the leadership baton to Joshua. Other examples are: Jesus Christ to Peter, Paul to Timothy and Elijah to Elisha. These were true leaders. Leaders see things differently from followers. They see opportunity in problems. They see success in failure. They envision a better future. Jesus Christ saw us redeemed while we yet sinners.

You are Carrying Your Destiny

Everybody is carrying their future in their hands, but millions of people think it is something that is far away. Your future is the next five minutes. It is the next five hours. It is the next five days. This looks like it is far but it is near. You are just like a seed that is just lying there but when it's planted and receives proper nutrients and sunshine, it will produce the tree.

The future is like a pregnant woman who has to go through nine months of pregnancy before giving birth to new life. During those nine months, it's difficult sometimes; she experiences morning sickness. It will require endurance and persistence. I recall when my wife was pregnant with our child. The pain or the experience of pregnancy was hard, but it was all worth it when she saw that beautiful baby for the first time.

The same applies to your development of your gift. You will need friendly people who will motivate and encourage you when there is pain, discomfort or challenges. You do not need toxic people or those who criticize you. Some people will be with you from the start of your process of development, but along the way, when things get rough, they quit and move on.

The Strategy for Entering into your Leadership Position

There is a saying, that "The beginning of everything is always difficult." You need to believe in yourself and trust God. You need to decide in your mind that you are going to make it be it business, project, marriage or education. Start by serving others with humility and sincerity. You will find people will become attracted to you and you will lead them.

Jesus Christ called only a few local boys from His hometown to follow Him. He told them to come with Him. Then He said to them, *"Follow Me, and I will make you fishers of men"* (Matthew 4:19). You might need to identify only a few people to help you start your mission and purpose, but in the long run, many will be attracted to you. Jesus Christ taught the disciples about the kingdom of Heaven and many people started to follow Him. In John 6, there is an account of Jesus feeding 5,000 men who followed Him.

For instance, my personal career and advancement were boosted when I continued to serve in all the organizations I was working with as well as seeking additional education. I kept doing my job with humility and pride, which gave me opportunities to serve at higher levels. You might become a great person, but whatever position you are serving, God knows about it and what happens next.

The Practical Steps for Leadership Development

1. Observe quiet time for prayer, reading, and meditation
2. Develop a leadership attitude.
3. Learn leadership qualities.
4. Identify your leadership mentors.
5. Commit to leadership ethics, values, and principles.
6. Develop a habit of meditation.
7. Apply those qualities in your life.
8. Learn how to coordinate and manage resources.
9. Begin to write down the pictures in your mind.
10. What kind of person do you want to become?
11. Write everything you desire.
12. Think about what you need to do to achieve it.
13. Write your passion.
14. Write your vision on paper.
15. Write down the goals you want to reach and give them a timeframe.
16. Stop reading books that are not related to leadership or your area of influence.
17. Look and study people around you.
18. Assess their attitudes towards your plans.
19. Identify the right people to work with you.
20. Look and take on opportunities that are linked to your dreams or leadership.
21. Design and develop a clear plan to do what you desire.
22. Seek advice if you cannot do it alone.
23. Accept guidance and counseling.

The Task for Aspiring Leaders

1. What plans does God have for me? Why did I come to the world? This questions will give you an indication of your purpose.

2. What will be the outcome or result of my life? What is my preferred future? These give you a vision of your preferred future.

3. What can you do to your purpose? What are you planning to do? How can you make it happen? Here you see your goals.

4. Why are you doing that? What motivates you? What are the reasons for doing that? Objectives.

5. How will you accomplish your goals? Where do you start? With whom? When? What is your plan?

6. What do you need to have? What resources do you have? Resources include (time, friends, family, funds, land, social networks and many more.)

7. Do you have a transparent approach? What is the roadmap? How long will it take you? What will be the possible obstacles?

16

Capture Your Leadership Vision

The most pathetic person
in the world is someone
who has sight but no vision.
Helen Keller

The Power of Leadership Vision

Are you a leader? Do you have a personal vision for your life? What about a corporate vision? If yes, is it from God? We have different kinds of people on Earth. There are those who are careless, careful, poor, rich, the have and have-nots. I believe a person without a vision is a problem person and therefore does not have an idea of where they are destined in life.

A person who has no vision is someone who cannot see beyond where they are at the moment. People without dreams are not good to live with because their interests are different from yours. The same is true for corporate vision. All organizations have visions they would like to see manifest. The vision is what makes an organization distinct from other organizations. A person without a vision is destined to personal failure. People without a vision will always be undisciplined. A true vision determines the course of the journey or destination.

Furthermore, a vision dictates what a leader and followers do and what they will not do. In other words, the purpose of a leader follows the vision. In my life, I have a vision for what I want to accomplish and transfer to the next generation. It is written and documented. My daily choices are guided by that vision. My vision determines my friends. My books are also related to my vision. My daily decisions are also connected to the vision. Each day, I do at least one thing that leads me to the vision I have documented.

God Showed me a Vision for my Future and Life's End

I recall a vision God showed me in 1997 about my past and future. God showed me where I had come from and I woke up sweating at 11 p.m., having gone to bed at 6 p.m. And 1 p.m., God showed me my future where I had wings and was flying, working with poor people and traveling to different places. At that time, I did not know fromw where I would start. But today, I am doing the things God showed me that I wrote down. Was it easy? No. Some of the places I have worked have been in conflict (environments) like Somalia. But if is God's vision, God will preserve you because it is according to His purpose. Proverbs 19:21 says, *"Many are the plans in the man's heart, but it is the Lord's purpose that will prevail."*

A vision statement is the most important and powerful statement that can be a source of great motivation and inspiration. If you have spent time alone, quietly, meditated, prayed and consulted God, you might be ready to document what you have on paper. You need to carry out the task and find answers to these questions. You need to write and re-write and review again and again until you are convinced spiritually and physically that is what you desire to do for the rest of your life.

A Dream is not the same as a Vision

Let me make it clear from the beginning. A vision is different from a dream. A lot of people have dreams. Even toddler's dream; that is why they wake up and cry. Sometimes they see things that scare them in their sleep. All humans are born with dreams and sometimes we can call them aspirations. We desire good things: good life, nice cars, houses, money. Desires are for individuals, but visions cause changes the conditions or lives of persons or groups. I believe a vision comes from God. A vision is an internalized picture of a preferred future or desired destiny. Moses was given a vision of a Promised Land in the desert. God told Moses, I want you to go and deliver the people from oppression and lead them to the Promised Land that I promised to their forefather Abraham.

A vision from God is always given to an individual, not a group. Moses was the only person that God spoke to about the Promised Land. No other human was present when God spoke with Moses. His brother Aaron joined Moses after God had already shared the information. Abraham was alone when God gave him a vision of his descendants being as countless as stars in heaven. Every true vision always has one believer, and that is the person who receives it. A true vision will result in changing the lives of people. If you are thinking about building a nice house, buy a car or have a fat bank account that is not a vision. It is called ambition.

God always wants the Vision Written Down

God knows that human beings live by what they see every day. He knows there is a limit to our intelligence. When God gives a leader a vision, the leader must write it down to make sure he doesn't forget it. Habakkuk 2:2-3 says,

> *Then the LORD answered me and said: 'Write the vision and make it plain on tablets, that he may run who reads it. For the vision is yet for an appointed time, But at the end, it will speak, and it will not lie. Though it tarries, wait for it; because it will surely come, it will not tarry.*

Here is a man who was in good fellowship with God. Habakkuk was a prophet, and God gave him instructions to write down the vision and make it plain. We should learn that when God gives a vision, it must be written down, documented and made accessible. If God can tell a prophet to write the vision, how much more should ordinary men and women follow Habakkuk's example?

It is the leader's responsibility to write the vision down. Leaders who will influence the world must have a clear vision and followers must be aware of the vision. In today's world, writing a vision is not as hard as it was years back. Leaders can decide to select a few followers to work and refine a vision and come up with what is called a vision statement. A vision statement is a one sentence summary of a preferred future or destiny.

In addition, God also wants His vision passed from one leader to the next one. In otherwords, a true vision from God can be transferred from one leader to another through mentoring. Once you have done your work efficiently, you freely transfer the vision to the next leader. Their are several examples of leaders such as David who transferred a vision to Solomon about building the temple.

Moses also transferred the vision to Joshua. Apostle Paul said these words in 2 Timothy 4:6-7 *"For I am already being poured out as a drink offering, and the time of my departure is at hand. I have fought the good fight, I have finished the race, and I have kept the faith."* When you have completed your assignment, such words will come to your heart. I remember listening to one of the interviews with Dr. Nelson Mandela. They asked him, do you have any regrets? He said No!

Correlationship of Vision and Purpose

As mentioned above, vision and purpose are interrelated. Let's take the example of Moses. God gave him the vision of the Promised Land in the desert. To fulfil this vision, he had to travel back to meet the Pharaoh in Egypt and tell him of his intention to lead the people to the Promised Land.

In the process of pursuing the vision, he met resistance. Pharaoh, after releasing the people, followed the Israelites with the armies of Egypt with the goal of bringing the slaves back. The same is true with you. You might be having a vision and some enemies want to stop you.

If it is a real vision from God, nobody will stop it. Pharaoh tried to stop the movement of people to the Promised Land, but he failed and was drowned. People will attempt to stop the visionary, but because the vision is from God, it cannot be prevented by circumstances, setbacks, problems, obstacles or challenges.

When Moses became an old man, he called the elders and transferred leadership to Joshua. Joshua worked with Caleb to advance the vision. Your vision should not die when you do. It should continue to improve the lives of others.

True Leaders Communicate their Vision to Followers

When Moses received a vision from God in the wilderness, his leadership was born. Moses followed God's instructions to go to the Pharaoh to release the people. When Moses followed the instructions, he began to accomplish his purpose.

To accomplish his purpose, Moses worked with Joshua and Aaron. A vision is not fulfilled by an individual but with a group of people who have the right attitude and commitment. You cannot accomplish a vision as an individual; it requires the support and ideas from others. When I conceived the vision of building a school for the poor children in my hometown, I could not do it alone, so I discussed it with my brother-in-law Simon Anguria. Today we have a school that helps children achieve quality education, and we are working to establish a leadership training center. Our vision is leaders are equipped and empowered to serve humanity and produce credible leaders for the next generation.

In addition, when a leader receives a vision, it is the responsibility of the leader to share it. Moses spoke about the vision for his team. It must be noted that leaders are responsible for communicating the vision to teams and followers. Without team ownership of the vision, it will be difficult to develop plans, goals or objectives to achieve the vision. True leaders always work with others to achieve the vision. A vision that is not shared or transferred will die with the visionary.

Furthermore, true leaders are not afraid of sharing their vision. Moses was never scared of Joshua. When the vision is communicated to followers, it motivates, inspires and energizes people. Leaders have an obligation to communicate the vision to followers.

Essential Features of a True Vision

1. Every vision is customized, distinctive and unique for every individual or organization.
2. Every vision is unique and revealed only to a single individual.
3. A vision is not given to a group, but it is fullfiled by people when it is captured by a leader.
4. A vision is achieved with people who believe in the leader and vision it self.
5. Every true vision produces a true leader.
6. Every vision has unique provisions from God.
7. Every vision will lead to changes in the situation or conditions of people lives.
8. Every vision is different from other visions.
9. Every vision requires self-discipline and obedience.
10. Every vision will come with its provision.
11. Every vision is inspired by God.
12. Every true vision does not create competition.
13. Every vision is concerned about the future.
14. Every vision is a preferred future and focused on the future.
15. Every true vision will be tested.
16. A visionary leader will be tested as well.

17

Know The Value of Integrity And Always Keep It

*The foundation stones for a
balanced success are honesty,
character, integrity, faith, love and loyalty.*
Zig Ziglar

Why Does Integrity matter in Leadership?

I believe that Integrity is the foundation of leadership. Integrity is more important than power and money. Followers want to see the leader manifest a true character where the leader is always true to himself. The integrity of a leader must be the same regardless of the weather conditions, events or circumstances. Leaders without morals or integrity are always destined to fail or lose their leadership positions.

Every year the world has been presented with stories of leaders who failed the integrity test. There is no need to mention names; you can check Google, CNN, BBC or any media plafform. Our world is crooked and consists of men and women with twisted character.

The leaders we are talking about are not only in government but in churches, the corporate world, sports, education, politics and almost every area of human endeavor. We have seen pastors, bishops, politicians, presidents, police officials, teachers, accountants, doctors, and sportsmen going to jail because of abuse of public resources, public trust and a lack of integrity.

Integrity protects leadership and legacy.

Integrity is the Only Protection of Leadership and Leaders

Leaders must be jealous of their integrity. They need to be responsible for everything they do and accept advice. No position should make a leader think or assume that they are important and do not need anyone. They should keep people around them that tell them their grey areas and take corrective actions. Inside every human is an internal compass that guide and ensure that right decisions are made. Leaders need to be vigilant and careful in keeping their character.

What is Integrity?

I would like to draw your attention to a statue of Kwame Nkrumah in front of Nkrumah Hall at Makerere University. Ever since I saw the statue in the 1990s, I can predict what kind of clothes it wears. The statue has been there for years without moving.

I bring in the idea of the statue to illustrate what integrity should be. The statue does not change, regardless of the environment conditions or seasons. Leaders must reach a point where their integrity is like a statue. They should never change, but instead they withstand all the pressures and conditions without losing their common sense and personal values.

The Effects of Deffective Character

Most of the problems in our world today originate from the broken walls of human character and cracks in integrity. There are several sad stories of great men or women who have destroyed their character, not only now but during Biblical times. Jacob stole from his brother. Abraham slept with a housemaid. Moses killed an Egyptian. Saul wanted to own wealth instead of obeying God's instructions. David slept with the wife of his commander. Samson slept with a Philistine woman, and you know the end of the story.

In our contemporary world, we might have read about Tiger Woods, the stories in the White House, President Bill Clinton and Jacob Zuma. Added to that are stories emanating from the Vatican about the molestasion of young children.

We saw how Zimbabwe, a great nation, nearly fell apart because of dictatorship. To me dictatorship is a character and integrity issue. All these issues are character and integrity issues. Can you imagine if all human beings were honest? How would the world look? That is why I say let the kingdom of God come quickly on Earth just as it is in heaven because in heaven there is integrity. There is holiness. There is absolute honesty. That is why we trust God. God is the same yesterday, today and forever.

What Does Character Mean?

When we talk of character, I want to bring an analogy of the alphabetical letters A, B, C, D, Z along with the integers 0, 1, 2, 3, 9. Each of these are called characters because they never change. A is always an A. The same is true with 2; it is the same even in China, Cuba, Cameroon or Comoros Island. The character is a quality of being stable, fixed and unchanging.

Having good character means having integrity. Character means you are the same throughout. What you say and do are the same at any time of the day. When your words contradict your actions, we say there is a lack of integrity. In other words, there is a character defect. The challenge that leaders are going to face is to keep their character. How you do it is simple. You need first to be accountable to God, family and trusted friends.

Each time I go to or visit Makerere University, the mere sight of Kwame Nkrumah's statue reminds me of character. Character means regardless of where you are, what you do must be the same even when nobody is watching you. If a leader wants to leave a legacy, they must protect their character. Samson died and left an unfortunate legacy. What will you say about Billy Graham when he goes to heaven? We will remember his character. What will you remember about George Bush, Bill Gates, or Bill Clinton? God himself does not change. God's nature is to be integrated and be one and God is three persons in one. It is called the Trinity.

Strategies for Protecting Good Character

There are many ways to preserve your character.

1. Seek First The Kingdom of God

Leaders need to seek the kingdom of God. Jesus spoke about this in Matthew 6:33. He said, *"Seek first the kingdom of God and all his righteousness."* Righteousness is a result of having no sin against God. The challenge is to avoid or eliminate sin. Sin also means a rebellion against God. A leader who wants to continue to influence others or followers must seek first God's kingdom. It will enable a leader to lead effectively. It will also help a leader achieve his vision and communicate it without any fear.

2. Avoid Bad Company or Groups of People

Paul, one of the early leaders of the church, wrote these words in 1 Corinthians 15:33-34 says: *"Do not be misled, bad company corrupts good character."* All human beings are born in the precious likeness of God, but the people we live or associate with are responsible for our character. These people could be your family, friends, peers, associates or workmates. Leaders must be careful of who becomes part of their company. If you are with bad company, your character will be dented and your leadership record may be damaged.

3. Standing Firm

Paul wrote about the price of keeping good character. *"And not only that, but we also glory in tribulations, knowing that tribulation produces perseverance; and perseverance, character; and character, hope"* (Romans 5:3-4). Paul told the Romans that regardless of the trials and tribulations, they should stand firm because when they persevere, their character will protect them. Going without money or poverty is not bad because if you are faithful, God will bless you with money. But if during the time of trial, you get into the habit of stealing, God will judge you (Hebrews 9:27).

4. Make Integrity the Number one Priority

Let people attack you but keep your integrity or character. You are going to face problems, tests, trials or tribulations including persecution, but maintain your integrity. Your honesty will open doors for your children, grandchildren, and generations to come.

5. Have Hope and Faith

When you are in the pit or prison or crisis, never compromise or exchange your character for material things. The story of Joseph in Genesis 41:41 is a wonderful example of a man who prevailed under difficult circumstance. Joseph's family attacked him and sold him to Egyptian merchants. In Egypt, he was jailed and later released to carry out his assignment. He ended up in the top office of the land. Why? He kept his character. Mr. Mandela was presented with several opportunities of freedom, but His conscience and integrity could not allow him to take those opportunities. What happened? He eventually led South Africa for five years and became a legend.

6. Know That God's Purpose Will Prevail

The greatest assurance I have in this life is found in Proverbs 19:21. *"Many are the plans in a man's heart, but it is the Lord's purpose that prevails."* This is the verse that has protected me from a teenager until this day as an adult. I never worry about what my future will be. I recall reading this scripture in the remote village of Bugiri in Uganda.

The final words are with God. That is why the Bible says God is the Alpha and Omega. Do not panic when things are not moving the way you want. You might want a nice house, car or status, and because of peer pressure, you engage in stealing, prostitution or robbery. You can die in the course of all those acts. But if you stay steady, God will open doors that nobody can close. I recall vividly my own life, when I had no car and all my friends were driving. I kept working hard, and as time went by, I grew in my career until I was able to buy cars. Today some of those friends are dead because they engaged in acts that destroyed their lives. They did not live to believe in God's final plans.

7. Believe There is a Time for Everything

King Solomon wrote there is time for everything. Ecclesiastes 3:1 says, *"To everything there is a season, A time for every purpose under heaven."* I love this verse so much that I apply it to all my daily situations. What I love with that statement is that everything is seasonal. Nothing remains constant. Everything will change. Your children will change. Your spouse will change. You will change. Your plans will change. You ideas will change. Your friends will change. Your team will change. Your education or knowledge will change. Your income or salary will change. The key to life is knowing that everything will change.

It is important to remember that nothing is permanent. Change will affect everything. When I am going through tough times, I am always at peace and have a high level of confidence that things will change. The advice I can offer is that you need to understand life. God gave His word in the Bible to teach us and know His mind. You might be in the pit right now. Remember, there is time for everything. Nothing lasts forever on Earth.

8. Determine to Build a Strong Foundation

Most of the houses that collapse under pressure have a weak foundation. Let us look at a child's education. If the early years are not handled carefully, the foundation will be weak. Gordon B. Hinckley said these words, "You can't build a high building on a weak foundation. You must have a solid foundation if you're going to have a high superstructure."

9. Keep Self-Discipline and Self-control

Keeping character requires self-discipline and commitment. A man or woman without faith will collapse when their character is tested. The protection of leadership requires loyalty to the goals, vision and plans.

There is no future for the man or woman who has no faith or for the unfaithful. Faithful people will be rewarded because faith is what pleases God. When you want to please God and receive His rewards, stay faithful. You cannot please God by singing, worshipping or praying in tongues or giving offerings. God demands humans to be faithful. He is interested in faithful servants.

10. Make Wise Choices and Decisions

Leaders must choose to build a strong foundation. Wise leaders are willing to take advice and apply it. The foolish one ignores the lessons. When I was a young adult, my desire was to build a strong foundation in my life. What I have been doing all my life is strengthening my internal character or foundation. You cannot build a strong foundation without sacrifice and investment. You have to learn to improve the foundation in all areas of life. The easiest illustration is the story of the wise and foolish builders in Matthew 7:24-29.

The Future of Leadership in World

The world is becoming a global village thanks to the inventors of the World Wide Web. Whatever happens in any corner of the world today will be known in a matter of seconds. For Instance, when the Ugandan Leader, Mr. Museveni stopped to attend a phone call at the roadside, it took seconds and the information was all over the media and all corners of the world. You can search about the story yourself on Google.

The future of leadership will be determined by men and women who will protect their integrity. Those leaders without morals will not have public trust. The top priority will be for leaders to study the value of character and how to protect it and ensuring proven integrity. There is no school or training where character is taught. The only thing that will protect a leader is the character. They can use power or resources, but in the long run, leadership will be lost if character is not guarded. I will write more on this in the next book on Building Leadership Character.

11. Make Humility a Top Priority

I believe this quality is no longer in existence in our world. The leaders have too much power and wealth. As such, they are proud and arrogant. They cannot be counselled and offered advice or guidance. They know it all. If you want to succeed as a leader, you must make humility a top priority. Be willing to listen and take advice.

18

Mentor Those Who Will Replace You

*Tell me and I forget, teach me
and I may remember,
involve me and I learn.*
Benjamin Franklin

Why Mentoring is Critical to Leadership and Succession?

This chapter talks about mentoring and training the next generation of leaders. Remember as a leader, you are a mortal being. The saddest thing in life is to watch success being destroyed because leaders neglect to mentor their replacements. If you are the leader of a political organization, business, company, institute or school, you need to take this very seriously. You will not be in that position forever.

I have heard people say, "No one can lead better than me." This might be true, but the reality in life is that change will come that could affect you. There is nothing on Earth that is as permanent as change. Change is said to be the only constant thing in life.

True Leaders Mentor Their Successors

When you study the life of Moses, you will notice that he prepared Joshua to take over after he was dead. Joshua was with Moses in many situations. He led the armies of Israel to war and participated in government meetings. When Moses was about to die, he introduced Joshua to the elders (Deuteronomy 31). Moses recognized his strength and announced that Joshua was to lead the people. How many leaders think like Moses?

Are you willing to let go of your political or business organization? Are you willing to give your ministry to another leader to continue? The Bible says Moses did it in Deuteronomy 31:7-8.

What True Leaders Do Differently

1. True leaders train the next leaders.
2. True leaders reproduce and develop the next leaders.
3. True leaders select among their followers who become the next leaders.
4. True leaders give others the opportunity to lead.
5. True leaders encourage the next leaders.
6. True leaders counsel the next leaders of what to expect and what to do. Moses told Joshua to be strong and courageous. What a message!
7. True leaders empower those who are weak to lead. Jesus did it with Peter and other disciples.
8. True leaders speak of what is coming and where they are going.
9. True leaders inspire the next leaders.
10. True leaders transfer vision through mentoring.
11. True leaders transfer power by empowering.
12. True leaders transfer their knowledge to their followers and next leaders.

Why Leaders Never Mentor Others

1. Leaders who have done evil things or actions are afraid to be discovered.
2. Insecurity. Our leaders are insecure in themselves. Their safety is in the power of a gun, not the word of God.
3. Greediness. They are greedy and never satisfied with the accumulated wealth or stolen wealth.
4. Some of the leaders are jealous when their followers perform better than they do.
5. Use of Greek ideas about leadership to control and manipulate followers.
6. Fear of facing the justice system to answer questions in relationship to their leadership.

The Next Generation:
What can Leaders do With It?

As I look at today's leaders several questions come to my heart. Are leaders preparing for tomorrow's leaders? The world we live is in need of leaders more than ever. Our world is facing challenges that need servant and self-motivated leaders. We need leaders who can plan and take the right decisions. We need leaders who are principled and not power hungry. We need leaders who have passion and a love for humanity. We need leaders who value human life. We need leaders who can transfer the vision to the next leaders. Leaders need to plan for succession.

The leaders of today will fade. If they think they are powerful, that is not true. Let the next generation find that our world is a peaceful one where the potential is released and maximised.

241

How to Select the Next Leaders?

A lot of leaders might be wondering how to carry out the responsibility of choosing the next leaders of their organizations. Jesus gave us a model that I believe is effective and can be reapplied.

Jesus Restores Peter

> So when they had eaten breakfast, Jesus said to Simon Peter, "Simon, son of Jonah do you love Me more than these?" He said to Him, "Yes, Lord; You know that I love You." He said to him, "Feed My lambs." He said to him again a second time, "Simon, son of Jonah, do you love Me?" He said to Him, "Yes, Lord; You know that I love You."
>
> He said to him, "Tend My sheep." He said to him the third time, "Simon, son of Jonah, do you love Me?" Peter was grieved because He said to him the third time, "Do you love Me?" And he said to Him, "Lord, You know all things; You know that I love You." Jesus said to him, "Feed My sheep. Most assuredly, I say to you, when you were younger, you girded yourself and walked where you wished; but when you are old, you will stretch out your hands, and another will gird you and carry you where you do not wish." This He spoke, signifying by what death he would glorify God. And when He had spoken this, He said to him, Follow Me. (John 21:15-19)

Jesus and Twelve Leadership Trainees

You are a leader and have been struggling with whom to select as the next leader. Jesus had a group of twelve leaders. He commissioned them and gave them authority as we saw in the story of the Great Commission. Do you see what Jesus asked Peter? He asked Peter a question of love. Thrice, Jesus asked him, *"Do you love me?"* Peter answered in the affirmative.

Why did Jesus ask a question concerning love? Think about it. You will remember this is the same Peter who said you are the Christ (John 6). This is the same Peter who got a knife and cut off the ear of one of the men who came to arrest Jesus. It is the same Peter who denied Jesus, but now Jesus is asking him, "Do you love me?" Jesus had his family, but He never asked any of them these questions.

Jesus never asked, "Do you have experience or are you intelligent? Are you capable of leading my group? Do you love the vision that I have? Do you want my authority?"

Jesus wanted someone who loves Him. When Peter confirmed and boldly said, "I love you," Jesus was able to know that He could carry out His mission. Jesus replied to Peter by saying "Feed my sheep."

If you are a leader who is struggling with choosing the next leader, use this model. Do not choose people who love your gifts, mission, vision or power. You should assess their degree of love for you. If they love you, they will carry on with your organization's vision. Do not think of blood relatives, think outside of your family and choose a leader who loves you and is willing to die for you.

Leadership Must not be Transferred to Relatives

Leadership is not by blood but by love. Peter risked his life to save his master. How many of the people that you have as a leader will do that? If you are a true leader, you need to pursue righteousness. If you ignore God's Word, destruction is certain. You can study David's word in Psalms 1:1-6.

True Leaders Develop a Leadership Team

True leaders take the opportunity to develop a leadership team that will carry on the great mission or great purpose and vision of a leader that departs. If you are a true leader who is committed to taking the people to the Promised Land, you must pursue the strategy to develop the next generation of leaders. Jesus Christ spent over three years developing a group of fishermen, tax collectors and taught them about His leadership philosophy.

He taught them about the kingdom, prayer, faith, love, giving, and many other relevant topics. He taught the disciples how to overcome problems, crises and advance the vision. When they were discouraged, He encouraged them.

In addition, when they had little faith, He taught them. Jesus gave the trainees an opportunity to lead and practice the knowledge He had imparted to them. He sent them out to cast out demons or heal the sick. Do you have people whom you have trained? Have they given you reports of their strong influence or leadership?

It must also necessarily be noted that the strategy of chosing twelve disciples is one of the most effective means of transferring leadership. Jesus Christ knew that large or big groups never change the world. The secret of true leadership lies on how they transfer leadership to a group of men and women who will capture the leader's vision but also love the leader.

19

Know Your Source Of Life

A people without the knowledge of their past history,
origin and culture is like a tree without roots
Marcus Garvey

The Power of Identity and Danger of Identity Crisis

There is nothing as bad as not knowing where you come from and your origin. I have heard of stories where children are born and do not know who their parents are. I have heard stories of adults who have written in to newspapers seeking to get in contact with their parents. There are many stories of individuals all over the world who are miserable because they are suffering from an identity crisis.

On the other hand, children without parents have challenges of identity. I read a story about former American President Barak Obama. In the 1980s, Mr. Obama traveled to Kenya and visited his father's birth place in Kogelo village. The purpose of the visit was related to knowing his roots in an attempt to get a real identity.

Many times I have asked people where they come from and the answer they give me is unique and an interesting one. For instance, one of the people I worked with in Somalia told me he came from South Africa. Another told me he was from Ghana while another said he came from Bangladesh. I think that the question of where one comes from is not linked to those answers. Yes, you could be coming from a particular country but is that enough? The question of identity is a serious question. It is probably the reason millions of people are engaged in activities that do not add value to their lives. An individual who does not know their identity needs help and must be helped.

What Was Jesus' Answer ?

Jesus was Who He was many times. He answered these questions wonderfully. On time Jesus said, *"I am the light of the world."* What does light do? Light dispenses away the darkness. Light brings life to normality. Light is a Hebrew word for knowledge. When you talk about knowledge in Hebrew, you are referring to light. If you have a person who is ignorant, it means he or she has no knowledge and no light. John 8:12 says, *"Then Jesus spoke to them again, saying, "I am the light of the world. He who follows me shall not walk in darkness, but have the light of life."* Darkness in Hebrew means ignorance. Jesus was saying when you follow Him you will not be ignorant, but instead you will acquire knowledge. Another time, Jesus was asked where was His Father? You can see the answer in John 8:18-20:

> *I am One who bears witness of Myself, and the Father who sent Me bears witness of Me. Then they said to Him, "Where is Your Father?" Jesus answered, "You know neither My Father nor Me. If you had known Me, you would have known My Father also." These words Jesus*

spoke in the treasury, as He taught in the temple; and no one laid hands on Him, for His hour had not yet come.

In John 6:35, we see, *"And Jesus said to them, 'I am the bread of life. He who comes to Me shall never hunger, and he who believes in Me shall never thirst.'"*

You can see that Jesus knew Who He was. An individual who knows his or her source is a stable person. One of the most important responsibilities for parents and guardians is to teach children their origin and identity.

Where is my True Origin or Source?

I might have been born to Earthly parents, but my true identity and likeness are from God, Who created me in His image. I carry in me God's character and quality. Genesis 1:26-28 taught me about my identity. It says let Us make man in Our image. The image is what I call identity. I came from the source of everything. God made me. I am not ashamed of God and being saved by Him.

Rita Akello

When you interact with many individuals, you might notice that they are afraid of their origin. I will tell you a story. When I was in high school, we were studying with boarding students and day scholars. I recall an incident with one of the girls who came with me from the same community. This lady, whom I refer to as Rita for purposes of this story, never wanted to be associated with her parents. One time her parents came to see her in the student's hostel in Mbale, and they came "loaded," meaning they came prepared with "goodies" for their daughter. I met the parents and led them to the hostel.

As the parents and I approached the hostel, the girl saw us and decided to tell her friends that she was not around and that we needed to leave the items or message at the gate with the watchman. The girl did not want her friends to know who her parents were and be identified with the peasants. The girl had told her friends that she came from a wealthy family. The girl, I believe, was suffering from an identity crisis and never wanted to relate with her parents.

Rita did the same thing when she went to college. She engaged in actions such as prostitution and sexual relationships with "rich or working class men." The aim was to get money to live at a certain level or status. The girl did not marry any of the men she was dating. Instead, she acquired HIV and later died at a young age with AIDS. What a sad story and tragic end. What killed Rita? I believe AIDS has no cure, but why could she refuse to be associated with her parents. The girl grew up in a rural setting and was able to get good enough grades to join a secondary or high school. The girl did not know who she was. She was not sure of her identity.

Today, there are millions of people like Rita, and sadly, they never know who they are. Knowing yourself and your identity and origin is an essential pillar of personal stability and confidence. I recall as a high school student, I went for examinations when I had no shoes. My friends and classmates laughed at me, and in many cases, I was using torn shoes or slippers or sandals. I was not ashamed or intimidated by my condition or temporary situation. I recall learning early in the Word of God that there is time for everything. There is a time when you have money, and there is a time when money will not be available. There is time to be healthy and time for sickness. There is time to have shoes and a time when there will be no shoes.

Ecclesiastes 3:1 says, *"To everything, there is a season, a time for every purpose under heaven."* My understanding and application of this text in my life enabled me to stand firm and not be intimidated. The key to life is knowing that life is seasonal and that nothing lasts forever. If you are down now, it does not mean you will be down forever. One day poverty will be history. If you are a president of a country, you should know it is not forever.

Things That do not Change

Through my study and research, I am convinced that there are only two things that do not change: God and God's promises. God does not change. God is the first and the last, the Alpha and Omega. God's Word does not change. God is the same yesterday, today and forever. When God makes or gives a promise, God will keep His word forever. For example, God promised Abraham a son as an heir. God fulfilled the promise after 25 years of waiting.

If God has given you a promise, you will need faith to receive it. Do you have faith? Do you trust in God's promises? The key to effectiveness in life is understanding that life is seasonal and seasons come and go. I know that you could be going throw a dark moment in your office, family, home or community. You need to recall that there is no permanent season. The season when you have dark moments and feel like quitting will also come to an end. Do not do something stupid that you will regret. Stay steady and believe that the season is passing. Stay steady and remain committed.

The Source of True Freedom is not a Government but God

As a teenager, I always wanted to be free from oppression and punishment. I have also heard people say they want to be free. Freedom is a state or the power or right to act, speak, or think as one wants without hindrance or restraint. It also means the absence of subjection to foreign domination or despotic government. Another meaning of freedom is the state of not being imprisoned or enslaved. Truth is the source of freedom not government, education or politics.

In my experience and search for liberty in life, I came to a Scripture that was a statement by Jesus Christ as to the source of liberty. John 8:32 says, *"And you shall know the truth, and the truth shall make you free."* No government can give you freedom, and if they do, it will be restricted. If a person offers you freedom, it can be taken away or revoked if the person feels you have become a threat.

Freedom comes from understanding that truth and its knowledge of the truth that gives you freedom. The truth is what I call principles. The source of freedom is truth. Something that is true does not change. Some people confuse the truth with facts. A fact is always different from the truth because facts change with time. For instance, scientists says the acceleration due to gravity is 10m/s. When an object goes up, it is believed it will come down. That is truth. Principles or truth are universal; they apply at all times. The key is knowing the truth. Psalm 15:2 says, *"He who walks uprightly, works righteousness, and speaks the truth in his heart."* When you live a life of righteousness and tell the truth, you will always be protected. Nothing protects you better than the truth. However, the facts always keep changing. The fact can be you dressed in a suit on Monday morning, but on Sunday you are using another type of attire. Facts are temporal whereas truths are eternal.

How Do you Know the Truth?

I believe truth comes from research. The word research is a prefix with two words "re" and "search." Research means to go back and search again or look for it again. That means it already exists but you have to search again to find it. The truth about God is found in His Holy Book, The Bible. The truth about a product is found in the manual. The truth is found in the mind of the maker of a product. That is why the Bible says God is truth. Until you discover the truth, everything around you will be false, and you will always search for the meaning of life in other people or associations.

It is Your Choice

I have come to appreciate that life is the result of the choices we make every day, and what is chosen today will determine what life we will have tomorrow. If you decide to read a book today, you have decided to add value to your life tomorrow. If you chose to drink today, you have decided to take a dangerous path of misery tomorrow. If you decide to engage in sexual relationships today, you have decided to lead a confused life.

During my life, I was confronted with awkward moments or situations that overwhelmed me and at times left me helpless and wondering. The decisions were about relationships with people that I treasured and valued so much. I also followed the teachings of Jesus Christ on loving your enemies and not judging others. I learned that these lessons were real in my life and I kept on forgiving those people who hurt me or my mind. I recall the attitude my grandparents had when my uncle, Charles Alfred Otuko, was killed in 1978. I was told how my grandfather, the late Aristebulo Michael Ongerep, would say that it is God who avenges and he died the same way. He too was murdered in cold blood.

20

Know The Power Of Value
And Scarcity

Try not to become a man of success,
but rather try to become a man of value.
Albert Einstein

The Principles and Lessons
From an Economic Class

During the economic class lesson, my economics teacher, Mr. Okumu Omuba in Mbale Secondary School in Eastern Uganda, introduced to us to the concepts that I believe every human being needs to know and understand. There were three major and critical concepts: scarcity, choice, and opportunity cost. I believe many students never understand the principles behind those terms. To me those three concepts became the " light and source of wisdom." I would like to offer my understanding of those terms and their applications.

What Does Scarcity Mean?

Scarcity is one of the fundamental economic problems of resources being limited in amount but desired in a seemingly infinite amount or unlimited quantities. For instance, the demand for money is never ending, but money is scarce. The demand for opportunities is unlimited, but opportunities are limited. The demand for jobs is unlimited, but jobs are not available for everyone on Earth. This means that human wants are infinite and limitless, but resources are limited. Let me put it in simple terms: people want more money, but money is not enough and available to everyone. Even the richest men like Bill Gates or Donald Trump has money, but they still have infinite desires that they are unable to satisfy.

Scarcity is the leading cause for our societies having insufficient productive resources to fulfill all human wants and needs. This situation requires people to make decisions about how to allocate resources efficiently to satisfy basic needs and as many additional wants as possible. In economics, scarcity refers to limitations – insufficient resources, goods, or abilities to achieve the desired ends. Figuring out ways to make the best use of or find alternatives is fundamental to economics.

What is Choice?

Choice always involves decision-making and selection. It can include judging the merits of multiple options and selecting one or more of them. Everything that happens in our lives is the result of choice. If we made the right decisions, then we made right choices. Life is a choice. Choice also means the act of choosing or the act of picking or deciding between two or more possibilities.

In all human existence, life is controlled by decisions and every person is a decision-maker. They make decisions to eat. They make decisions on what to wear. They make a decision on who becomes their spouse. They make decisions what schools their children will attend. Which university will they go to study? They decide who their friends become. I believe decisions not only determine life, but also they have the power not to make decisions.

God created all humans with the power to make choices and decisions based on their will. A will is not a good power but also dangerous a power. This means the humans have the power to decide what happens on the plannet. A will allows us to make choices, either good or bad. Humans can decide on anything they want. The choice is always in our hands. That is why I can say with boldness that success is a choice. Failure, however, is also a choice.

I do not believe in luck. I was conscious of actions that would affect my destiny. The difference between successful people and those that fail are the choices and decisions they have made over time.

What protected me was my vision. I had a personal vision of helping my family. I had to discipline myself because I knew if I began drinking, my vision or plans would fail. There is a saying I had when I was doing monitoring and evaluation work in UNICEF: "If you do not know the road you are taking then any way can lead you to a destination that you might not want to follow." A person who has a personal vision is capable of success, but it requires several other attributes like prayer, discipline, hard work, commitment, focus, dedication, faith, and a favorable environment and the company of friends with a positive attitudes.

What are Opportunity Costs?

The third concept is opportunity cost. It sounds so simple, but it is a powerful concept. An opportunity cost refers to a benefit that a person could have received, but gave up, to take another course of action. Let us state it differently: an opportunity cost represents an alternative given up when a decision is made.

In everything people do, there is an opportunity cost. In every decision there is a cost and a benefit. Some decisions have significant consequences while others have secondary effects. Some decisions cause minor problems and other major problems. It is sometimes the choice of the person on how to solve the problems and avoid them becoming pathological. For instance, some people start smoking cigarettes at an early age, which I consider minor problems; but with time, they become major problems leading to a pathological crisis.

Why Value and Scarcity Necessary?

While studying economics, our teacher explained that the more common the product or service, the cheaper it is. Alternatively, the more common goods are in the market or industry, the cheaper they are. This is known as the law of supply and demand. For you to become a success in your generation, you need to increase your value. Scarcity makes the product valuable. Even when a product has been made, the value must be added to increase its economic value.

Gold, silver, oil or diamonds are valuable in the marketplace because they are rare or not common. Using that analogy, any human with a desire to become valuable must become scarce and uncommon. When you become rare, you will become significant. When you become rare, people will look for you, just like the way gold, silver among others are dug. These precious metals are dug because they are rare, expensive and valuable. But how do you become valuable? You become rare and unique. Refine your talents and gifts, master something, and excel in it. I always want to tell people that "do not become a jack of all trades." In my own life, I have no desire of studying anything other than only two area: leadership and management.

Actions for Increasing Personal Value

There are several measures and decisions you will need to do to increase your value.

1. Personal investment and development: Leader must invest in themselves and those who follow them. This could be through training, coaching, mentoring or professional development.

2. A leader must always be determined. Leaders must chase after their purpose and move with followers to the unknown.

3. Sometimes you need to review and assess the kind of people you associate with. You might need to change some of your friends and invest by identifying people that influence you.

4. You might also need to change your library or the books that you read. Buy books that have solutions and ideas to the problems that are affecting you.

5. Become a consultant in an area where people seek your opinion, views, and advice.

6. Try to do something you have never done. You might discover new insights and learn some experiences that become valuable. Otherwise, you will not become valuable.

7. You need to have a clear focus of your destination. It will serve as a roadmap. It will dictate your choices, priorities, and decisions.

8. Stop wasting time, but spend time doing something valuable. Wasted time is life lost. Invested time is invested life.

9. People will not look for you because of your looks or appearance, your value is what makes you worthy and valuable.

10. Take advantage of every opportunity that God gives you to refine your gifts, increase the value, and economical price.

How to Carry Out Self-Assessment?

I have worked in large humanitarian organizations of the United Nations. While in those entities, I observed and participated in several assignments. There were moments of work, planning, along with internal and external evaluations. There were moments of mid-term or mid-year reviews. During those excercises, the organization would decide what is working or what is not working. Also, what needs to be maintained or what needs to be discountinued. If such organizations can carry out these actions, what about individuals? I believe that every person needs to carry out a mandatory self-assessment on regular basis.

Effective living requires personal dedication to a personal evaluation and critical self-assessment. If you are serious about effective living, then the following questions should serve as a guide and reminder:

1. What are your strengths?
2. What are your weaknesses?
3. What are the threats facing you?
4. What opportunities do you have?
5. What actions are you doing not connected to your destination?
6. With whom are you associating?
7. Are they helping you to achieve your desired goals?
8. Do you know what you want in life?
9. What difference do you intend to make in this world?
10. Who are you?
11. What do you want?
12. Where are you going?
13. Where did you come from?
14. What keeps you going and focused?
15. What motivates you?
16. What excites you?
17. How is your private life?

Things That Give You Influence on Earth

There are eight specific things that give you influence. If you do not have any of these things, you will always be influenced and dominated. Your goal must be to acquire these things rightfully:

1. **Wealth:** A person who has wealth and riches has influence over those without wealth and riches.

2. **Property owned:** The people who have properties will always dominate those without such properties. However, you must question how those properties were acquired.

3. **Knowledge:** Those with knowledge or expertise in a given field or career will have influence in that area. If you have no knowledge, you will have no influence. You will always be influenced by other peope. They decide for you in areas that affect you.

4. **Gifts:** Those with special gifts and talents will have authority and influence.

5. **Control of systems:** People who have control of systems such as parties, organizations, corporations or associations have influence.

6. **Control of media and resources:** A person who has control of public media, resources and other assets will participate in decisions without you.

7. **Specialization:** A person who has specialized in a particular area or training such as medicine, law, education, leadership will have influence.

8. **People:** A person with many followers will control and influence society.

God's Courtroom

The critical point is that if you are going to obtain any of this and use it to influence your generation, it must be secured with integrity and honesty. Anything that is illegally acquired will bring a curse to you and your children up to the fourth generation. God will judge you and your offspring. What will happen to you and all leaders is summarized in Hebrews 9:27.

21

Develop a Plan For Your Future

Nothing in all the world is more
dangerous than sincere ignorance
and conscientious stupidity.
Dr. Martin Luther King Jr.

The Greatest Enemy of man is Ignorance not Satan

I believe that the greatest enemy of man is not the devil, but ignorance or lack of knowledge or wisdom. There are millions of people who blame their problems on other people, their leaders, teachers or family background. Through research, I now tend to disagree. To me, ignorance and stupidity are the worst enemies of humanity. For instance, if you or your children are ignorant, you will be destroyed by the forces of change, nature, globalization, or evil forces. God created human beings with brains, but a lot of them have empty minds. Alcohol has destroyed many brains. Some have been contaminated and have stored useless knowledge. This makes life difficult for most people.

I was asked to coordinate a very high-level meeting at Safari Park Hotel in Nairobi. I met a group of workers who were to work with me for the overall coordination and organization of the meeting.

They spoke about the devil leading people astray, and I listened to them. One of them said that when they went to the streets, it was the devil. I tried to puncture their arguments by asking how they came to the place we were. I asked them again who chose the clothes, shoes, etc. that they were wearing. They answered they decided. I explained to them that the devil does not decide for them to go to the streets: it is their personal decisions and choices.

To become a leader is not a difficult thing because all humans were created by God to dominate. It is a personal choice and decision. Beginning today, you can decide what you will do with your life. The only reason why we have so many followers is that people lost their dominion power during the fall of man in the Garden of Eden in Genesis 3. If you have a desire to lead, you must memorize and master the following keys by heart, live by them, and then practice them all your life. Never forget or ignore these keys because they are the source of your leadership and influence. If you ignore these keys, your leadership has a shelf life and your influence will be canceled.

The Steps in Planning for Your Leadership and Future

1. Discover Your Original Purpose

God creates everything for a purpose and to fulfill a purpose. You need to ask God to reveal to you your purpose and vision. What is your reason for existence? Why did God create you? Do what God created you to do. Do not attempt to do everything.

2. Capture Your Vision

You need to picture your preferred destiny of your life. Do you have plans that will lead you to that desired destination? Who can help you accomplish that purpose so that you reach the vision? Your vision will inspire you, and it will come to pass and God's plans will be done. I have a personal vision for my life, and I review it every day. I memorize it.

As an example, this is what I am striving toward:

My Vision Statement

Aspiring and credible leaders are equipped and empowered to serve humanity.

Purpose Statement

To equip and empower aspiring and credible leaders to serve humanity.

Core Values

- Accountability and faithfulness.
- Decency, persistence and patience.
- Commitment to continuous learning.
- Integrity and honesty.
- Respect and humility.
- Service and hard work.

3. Discover and Exploit the Potential in You

You will have to carefully assess and examine the abilities, skills, knowledge, resources and gifts that you have and begin to refine them. You have limitless abilities and hidden gifts that you are not using rightly. You are like a seed; there is a tree inside a seed. Work so that you can manifest your potential. God had everything including the universe inside of Him. You are built with potential.

4. Develop Goals of Your Purpose to Achieve Your Vision

You should spend time coming up with clear goals to achieve your vision. Goals and activities must be decided to help you achieve the vision. Consult people if you have no idea on how to do it. Also, think of a road map, a plan and strategy to achieve your goals.

5. Maintain and Maximize Your Passion

You will need to be persistent, resilient, and consistent, and with prayer, you will continue to cultivate and nurture that burning desire to achieve your purpose. You need to keep a spirit of prayer if you are going to maintain your passion. You need to develop and persistently remain focused on the vision that you have.

6. Be a Person Who is Trustworthy

You will need to gain people's trust and confidence in you and your beliefs. You must work to build trust in other people. The trust comes from being consistent and keeping your commitments and promises. If you run into problems, communicate and apologize where you fail to live up to the promises.

7. Preserve Your Integrity

You have to guard and protect this core element and have good motives, just as God the Creator is Holy and Faithful. You need to guard your mind against corrupt and wrong ideas and motives. Keep your heart from the things that can destroy and distract your life and plans. You will always face temptations to do evil but stay on course. Always look at the vision that God has placed in your heart. You need to check to make sure the vision is from God. A vision from God is not self-centered but helps others become better. God gave Moses a vision in the wilderness to benefit the oppressed people, not Moses or Joshua. I do all I can to do the right thing amidst the temptations to take shortcuts.

8. Set High Standards and Values While Defining Your Principles

There are things you believe and these things you will not break or compromise. Learn and nurture self-discipline, self-regulation, self-awareness and self-management. Values will protect you. Stay close to your principles. Principles are more permanent than problems. Problems will come that will try to get you to discard your principles. Stay the course, and your principles and values will save your life.

9. Develop Your Faith in God as You Pursue Your Goals

Put your trust in God, praying and reading God's word. You must have unwavering faith that God will fulfill His purpose for the life He gave you as you lead. You need to have faith in God's promises. Philippians 1:6 says, *"Being confident of this very thing, that He who has begun a good work in you will complete it until the day of Jesus Christ."* God will not abandon His plans but He will abandon you if you abandon Him. If you seek Him, you will find Him, and He will fulfill His purpose.

10. Take Risks and Become an Explorer of the Unknown

Be willing to fail. If you are going to fail, fail big. Trust God. If you fail, do not give up; keep trying and learn any lessons from failure. Failure gives you an opportunity to grow and learn. Ask for help from family or friends if you need it.

Also, you need to explore at great lengths the ideas, plans, and dreams that you have and identify the people and resources that are required so you can serve the gift to this generation and your world. If you have the dreams, ideas or things that you want to do, take risks to carry them out. There might be some people in the world with resources that will help you achieve that dream.

11. Become a Servant of Others

Serve your gifts with humility to those around you and practice servant leadership at all times. Everywhere you find yourself, be a servant and get involved in serving. Do not wait to be served but serve those around you. However, being a servant is the most difficult thing I have ever found in people because people want to be bosses.

I recall a time when I was serving as an usher welcoming dignitaries and leaders from several organizations who were working my employer. The next week, I was invited to have lunch with the Country Director of DFID. It was a privilege. Service gave me this opportunity, and we discussed a couple of things which impacted my life. Are you willing to serve?

The Qualifications Required of Effective Leadership

Paul was an apostle who led the early church. He wrote a letter to Timothy, a young pastor he had mentored. The summary of the letter is in 1 Timothy 3:1-13. That passage lists the qualifications Paul gave for overseers and deacons. Overseers are another word for a leader, a supervisor or administrator.

Paul's teaching on qualifications of overseers or leadership positions are as follows:

> *This is a faithful saying: If a man desires the position of a bishop, he desires a good work. A bishop then must be blameless, the husband of one wife, temperate, sober-minded, of good behaviour, hospitable, able to teach; not given to wine, not violent, not greedy for money, but gentle, not quarrelsome, not covetous; one who rules his own house well, having his children in submission with all reverence (for if a man does not know how to rule his house, how will he take care of the church of God?); not a novice, lest being puffed up with pride he fall into the same condemnation as the devil. Moreover, he must have a good testimony among those who are outside, lest he falls into reproach and the snare of the devil. (1 Timothy 3:1-7)*

The Qualifications for Leadership

Any individual or person who desires to lead and take up leadership position must have the following qualifications:

1. Be faithful in all areas or things (e.g., money, wealth, power).
2. Be blameless or righteous.
3. Be temperate, pleasant, self-controlled and a lover of peace.
4. Be sober and not a drunkard.
5. Exibit good behavior, character, and personality.
6. Be able to teach followers.
7. Be hospitable, friendly, welcoming, social and cordial.
8. Exibit non-violent and peaceful in approach to life and challenges.
9. Be generous and not greedy for money and wealth.
10. Does not engage in quarreling and coveting other people's possessions.
11. Knows how to lead, rule his or her family and have children who submit and obey.
12. Be humble and practices humility.
13. Has a testimony of righteousness.
14. Be tested and proven as trustworthy.
15. Be a person of integrity and honesty.

Message To Our Leaders

The best message that I believe all leaders must accept is that no leader will rule or govern forever. The time will come when you will no longer be a president, governor, senator, parliamentarian or counselor. When this times comes, leaders must transfer leadership. There is also no leader who is above need for counsel or guidance.

You might not have realized that you have made bad decisions and that your decisions have cost the nation or corporate organization resources or even cost some people their lives. You might not be bothered about all this, and you are now powerful. You have wealth and everything that you need and want, yet millions are suffering and are impacted by your actions.

There is a simple step that you need to do. You need to take a bold decision and repent to God. You need to ask God to forgive you for the sins you have committed as a leader. When you ask for forgiveness through repentance, God is faithful to forgive your sins. Even King David, after committing the terrible sins of murder and adultery, repented to God. David was a king of Israel, but the Holy Scripture says He sought God's repentance in Psalm 51. The words of David in that Psalm show and demonstrates his failings, struggles in life, and his sinful nature. This shows you are not the only leader who has fallen short. There are thousands of leaders who are also struggling with the same problems or sin you face. Even as the author of this book, I acknowledge my sins, mistakes, and foolishness before God. I seek God's forgiveness every day. You too must do likewise.

If you want God to forgive your sins and pardon you, then you have to pray a special prayer. Prayer is about you establishing a personal relationship with Him. God is faithful, holy, merciful and mighty. We trust God because of His faithfulness and holiness, and His stable nature. If God were not faithful, nobody would trust God. But God is the same yesterday, today and forever. There is no one that can even come close to being like God.

God's powerful word of Scripture that is chosen for you is from prophet Isaiah.

Read this:

> Remember this, keep it in mind, take it to heart, you rebels. Remember the former things, those of long ago; I am God, and there is no other; I am God, and there is none like me. I make known the end from the beginning, from ancient times, what is still to come. I say, "My purpose will stand, and I will do all that I please." (Isaiah 46:8-10)

Salvation Prayer

Dear Heavenly Father and God of All Creation: You created and manufactured my life for a purpose, and without any mistake, I am aware that You created me to perform and fulfill my purpose and You desire that in me. I know that I have fallen and disobeyed Your laws and principles, and now I have lost my sense of direction and purpose in life.

I am also aware that your Son Jesus Christ is the way, the truth, and life, and without Him, I can do nothing. I believe that with Him, I will discover my purpose. I, therefore, ask You in the Name of Jesus to cleanse my life and send your Holy Spirit to dwell in my life and heart to reveal my purpose and fulfill it and live effectively. I surrender to Jesus Christ as my personal Savior and my Lord, and I commit 100% to do Your will and fulfill my purpose that You created me to finish. In the name of Jesus Christ, I have prayed. Amen.

If you have sincerely prayed this prayer, please write to me using the following address and share your commitment with me.

We also offer training, coaching, mentoring, seminars and workshops on leadership, purpose, overcoming crises and vision among many areas.

Dr. Samuel Odeke, DSL
C/O CTSL Uganda
P.O.Box 34820 Kampala, Uganda or
P.O.Box 2648 Mbale, Uganda
Telephone: +256783563417/782276765
E-mail: samuel.odeke@yahoo.com
Website: www.samuelodeke.com

About The Author

Dr.Samuel Odeke, was born in a polygamous, poor family and neighbourhood. He is the first born from a dozen children from three mothers. His parents served as civil servants. He attended rural primary schools, before joining high school and later Makerere University.

Dr. Samuel Odeke earned a Doctorate of Strategic Leadership with specialization in Strategic Leadership from Regent University in 2017. He received an M.A. in Organizational Leadership and Management from Uganda Christian University. He also holds a Post Graduate Diploma in Public Administration and Management and Masters of Management with Specialization in Public Administration and Management from Uganda Management Institute. Earlier, he received a Bachelor of Science Degree and Post Graduate Diploma in Education from Makerere University.

Dr. Odeke serves in various capacities such as an international civil servant, humanitarian worker, speaker, teacher, educator, leadership and management mentor and consultants for both private and public organizations. He travels to different countries attends and facilitates international conferences, seminars, and workshops. To him leadership and management are two critical areas that need to be addressed if humanity is to achieve its purpose in life and release it potential. World problems are a result of bad leadership and poor management.

Dr. Odeke has worked with large humanitarian and development organizations among others such as World Vision, United Nations World Food Programme (WFP), United Nations Children's Fund (UNICEF) among others. He has travelled in different countries such as Kenya, Rwanda, South Africa, Nigeria, Belgium, Spain, Netherlands, and the United States. Dr. Odeke believes that leadership can be developed through empowering, coaching, training and mentoring. He is a member of International Leaders Association (ILA), The Christian Book Sellers Association (CBA) and Africa Strategic Leadership Forum (ASLF).

Dr. Odeke has a very humble background. He is married with children. He experienced tragedy when he lost his mother at age 14, his grandfather at 15, and grandmother at 18. Those traumatic events and experiences changed his perception of life. As a result, he began to search for answers related to life. As a teenager, Dr. Odeke also witnessed the impact of war, conflict and massive cattle raids in his district of Bukedea (formerly part of Kumi District) in the late 1980s, where hundreds of lives and properties were lost. Many times he survived death from both government soldiers and rebels.

Dr. Odeke has applied these principles he learned through education despite becoming an orphan as a teenager after the mother's early death. Dr. Odeke is an inspiration and influence to many of his generation. He uses these principes, you too can make a difference in your generation.

www.ingramcontent.com/pod-product-compliance
Lightning Source LLC
Chambersburg PA
CBHW060335200326
41519CB00011BA/1941